PUTNAM 'N I!!

THE
German Soldier
IN WORLD WAR II

THE
German Soldier

IN WORLD WAR II

Dr. S. Hart, Dr. R. Hart and Dr. M. Hughes

MBI Publishing Company

This edition first published in 2000 by
MBI Publishing Company,
729 Prospect Avenue, PO Box 1, Osceola, WI 54020-0001 USA

MBI Publishing Company books are also available at discounts in bulk quantity
for industrial or sales-promotional use. For details write to Special Sales Manager
at Motorbooks International Wholesalers & Distributors, 729 Prospect Avenue,
PO Box 1, Osceola, WI 54020-0001 USA.

Library of Congress Cataloging-in-Publication Data Available.

ISBN 0-7603-0846-2

Editorial and design: Amber Books Ltd
Bradley's Close, 74-77 White Lion Street,
London N1 9PF

Editor: Vanessa Unwin
Design: Graham Curd

Printed and bound in Italy

Picture credits:
The Robert Hunt Library: 29, 60-61, 63, 64-65, 67, 68-69, 95, 98-99, 155, 156-157, 159.
TRH Pictures: 2-3 (Imperial War Museum), 6-7, 8, 9, 10, 12, 13, 14-15, 16, 17, 18-19, 20-21, 22-23, 24,
25, 26-27, 28, 30, 32-33, 34-35, 37, 38, 40-41, 42, 45, 46-47, 48-49, 51, 52, 54-55, 56, 57, 58, 62, 66, 71,
72-73, 74, 75, 76, 78-79, 80, 82, 83, 84, 86-87, 88, 89, 90, 91, 92, 93, 96-97, 101, 102, 103, 104-105, 106,
107, 108, 110-111, 113, 114, 117 (IWM), 118, 119 (IWM), 120-121 (IWM), 122-123, 125, 126, 127, 128,
129, 130, 132, 135, 136-137, 138, 139, 140-141, 143, 144-145, 146, 147, 149, 150-151, 152, 153, 154,
158, 160, 162-163, 164, 166, 167, 169, 170-171, 172, 173, 174-175, 176-177, 178, 180, 181, 182-183,
184 (US Army), 187, 188-189.

Page 2–3: A German mortar detachment in Stalingrad prepare to move off.

Contents

Moulding the Soldier

After 1935, service in the German armed forces (*Wehrmacht*) was compulsory and the majority of those who fought during World War II did so as conscripts. Most enlistees joined the Army in preference over the Air Force and the Navy. In order to serve in the military, a recruit had to be physically and mentally fit, with no serious criminal record, and had to be a German citizen. Germany was a militaristic society and its citizens rarely viewed conscription as an onerous infringement of civil liberties: rather, most Germans viewed it as an honourable and proud obligation to the state and the German people (*Volk*). Indeed, members of the armed forces invariably received deference from civilians and were usually held in high social esteem. It was unusual, for instance, to see a young German soldier on leave without a number of female admirers, for the state officially defined military service as a duty of honour rather than one of obligation.

A minority of recruits volunteered for service before they were called up. Undoubtedly the knowledge that they would eventually be conscripted prompted some to volunteer first; others volunteered for patriotic reasons or under family and peer pressure to 'do their bit'. Men called to service had, for the most part, already received some pre-military training. Many recruits already had completed a term, usually of six

Left: The colours are presented by an honour guard at a German Army parade. Although only symbolic, each unit was very proud of its colours.

months, in the State Labour Service (*Reichsarbeitsdienst*) where they had performed construction and labouring duties in a quasi-military environment. Here individuals learned drill, marching, discipline and unit camaraderie. Other recruits had served as air force anti-aircraft auxiliaries assisting at flak batteries or received some military preparatory training in the Hitler Youth movement.

Those most likely to volunteer were the young who had grown up under National Socialism and who, for the most part, knew little and cared less for the outside world. This Nazified youth often proved to be the most fanatical – though frequently also not the most long-lived – German soldiers. Paul Kammberger was one such ardent young Nazi who advanced through the various branches of the Hitler Youth movement as a teenager until, in 1943, he eagerly volunteered, aged 17, to join the 12th SS Panzer Division *Hitlerjugend* then forming in Belgium. Enlisting was, after all, the most exciting adventure of a

Below: The 92-year-old Field Marshal von Mackensen, a hero of World War I, was a firm supporter of Hitler.

young German boy's life, Kammberger recalled, but for many it proved to be a fatal adventure.

Training

Once called up, a recruit underwent basic training that was long, arduous, and realistic. German training programmes did not restrict themselves to an eight-hour day between the hours of nine-to-five, but sought to replicate as closely as possible combat conditions. Troops trained in all weathers and during the evening and night. Basic training was inherently dangerous since live-fire exercises were routine in order to recreate combat conditions that were as realistic as possible. Troops were therefore exposed to real danger of death on the proving grounds of Germany. Indeed, the German military accepted the one per cent fatality rate it suffered in training as the necessary price to pay for saving more soldiers' lives later on the battlefield. After all, it was better to remove the incompetent and the reckless in training than suffer their liability on the battlefield. Training was also forward-looking and thorough, in that every soldier was instructed to do his superior's job as well as his own in case they had to assume command. Hans Werner was one such typical wartime conscript called up in 1940. Describing his training experiences in letters home to his family, he commented that the food was basic but available in plenty, and that personal hygiene and cleanliness was constantly stressed, much to his chagrin. Training was long and hard, and discipline rigidly enforced, he wrote. But what Werner remembered above all was the bonding – the sense of group identity – that the challenges of basic training forged. For the first time in his life, Werner admitted, he now felt that he truly belonged to something that he was proud to be a part of: the mighty *Wehrmacht*.

Doctrine

At the heart of German training was the inculcating of a progressive, universally taught doctrine: a set of basic assumptions, beliefs and operating instructions that all German troops, irrespective of service, learned and were expected to follow. Adherence to this modern, uniform and

Above: Five recruits, dressed in fatigues, practise how to march in step by linking arms together at a German training camp before the war.

realistic doctrine, enshrined in the 1936 *Truppenführung* (Troop Leadership) manual, was one of the great strengths of the German Army. Developed in the early 1930s by some of the Army's best minds, it avoided the parochialism inherent in individual service doctrines and represented a holistic set of procedures for the Army as a whole. The soundness and forward-looking nature of this doctrine made a significant contribution to the military triumphs Germany achieved in the early years of World War II.

Among the basic principles of German doctrine was due emphasis on individual leadership and initiative. The *Truppenführung* emphasised what the Germans termed mission-oriented tactics. That is to say, doctrine expected senior commanders to give subordinates broad orders but to leave the actual implementation of those orders to the discretion and experience of subordinates. Such an approach provided maximum flexibility and initiative. Junior officers did not simply learn 'school' solutions to the problems they might encounter but were instead taught to think for themselves, to apply their military knowledge and expertise, to have confidence in their own decisions, and to act upon them.

In contradiction to the stereotype of the German soldier as a blindly obedient automaton, the *Truppenführung* emphasised not only individual initiative but also offensive verve. Doctrine rightly ascribed the attack to be superior to the defence and insisted that speed and surprise could often allow an outnumbered and outgunned attacker to prevail over a stronger enemy. The system worked very well in the early war years when the cream of German society fought and confronted western militaries still struggling with the crippling effects of the Great War. Such flexibility and initiative contributed in no small part to the devastating German military triumphs early in the war, as junior officers and NCOs were conditioned to seize opportunities that presented themselves on the battlefield without the lengthy delay in seeking higher approval. But as the war progressed and Germany suffered enormous casualties, the quality of leadership inevitably declined since training standards slipped. Consequently, commanders became more and more inexperienced, resulting in increasing examples of tactical ineptitude. At the same time, Germany's enemies had developed military proficiency and it became harder to achieve the kind of tactical successes at low cost which had been routinely achieved early in the war.

The repulse of the 9th SS Armoured Reconnaissance Battalion at the Arnhem road bridge on 18 September 1944 during the Allied 'Market Garden' offensive exemplifies the potentially disastrous consequences of a doctrine that emphasised offensive action and individual initiative. That morning, the battalion commander, *SS-Hauptsturmführer* (Captain) Viktor Gräbner made a fatal decision to attack the bridge by coup de main. Disdaining the resistance potential of the lightly armed British paratroopers opposing him, Gräbner adhered to the tenets of the *Truppenführung*: that swift offensive action using speed and shock could overcome a numerically superior enemy entrenched in strong defences. However, adherence to the *Truppenführung* doomed Gräbner and many of his men to death that morning. Gräbner personally led his armoured column to seize the bridge, but within minutes, intense British fire had decimated his force, with Gräbner falling at the head of the col-

Below: German soldiers snatch some rest in a cornfield whilst training. Note the field binoculars that some of them carry.

umn. The doctrine of no other western military, save perhaps the Red Army, would have encouraged the kind of bold, offensive verve that failed so spectacularly on the Arnhem bridge that day.

Discipline

The German Army maintained order, discipline and combat effectiveness through a draconian system of military justice in which even minor offences could meet with severe punishment. Given its history, particularly the very late emergence of a united German nation in 1870, twentieth-century German culture was inherently deferential to authority and obedient to its leaders, both political and military. It was thus a society where many people put national unity and strength foremost and before individual liberties and freedoms. This culture recognised the need for discipline in an effective military force.

A soldier might be disciplined for infractions of the German military code of justice via a progressive series of punishments that started with docked pay and lost privileges for minor infractions and which ascended through barrack arrest, special duty (such as extra guard duties or fatigues), deduction of pay, to loss of rank and imprisonment. The German authorities might incarcerate more serious or repeat offenders in a military prison in the field or in the home military district. However, another common punishment was temporary assignment to a dreaded penal battalion. Such units were invariably assigned the most difficult and dangerous combat missions. Their task was to attempt to rehabilitate offenders, allowing them to return to the army proper. 'Rehabilitation' could be achieved in several ways. One way was survival through the period of assignment to the unit, which was quite difficult, given the dangerous, often suicidal, missions penal units undertook. Consequently the 'easiest ticket' out of a penal unit was often via exceptional feats of battlefield heroism through which a soldier could regain his military honour and return swiftly to the army proper.

German military justice was also prone to convict soldiers accused of infractions of the military code of justice. During the first two years of World War II, for instance, 89 per cent of German soldiers brought to trial were convicted by military courts. Officers, naturally, were more likely to be acquitted – indeed, 23 per cent were – because the emphasis on officer leadership and initiative necessitated greater willingness to give officers the benefit of the doubt. The German military also demonstrated a willingness to execute its own, especially as the war progressed. While the precise number of those soldiers judicially murdered by the Nazi regime will probably never be known, the total came close to 30,000. As the war progressed, military justice became more erratic and murderous as the Nazi regime added the nebulous crime of 'undermining fighting spirit' as a capital offence alongside murder, rape, homosexual acts, desertion, mutiny, treason, and assaulting a superior officer. By 1945 flying courts martial (like the SS *Feldjäger*) travelled around arresting troops wandering around the rear and executing them after drumhead trials. While many of those executed were deserters or shirkers, at least some were highly decorated, loyal frontline soldiers who just happened to be in the wrong place at the wrong time.

This was the fate that befell *Hauptmann* (Captain) Hellmut Schmidt, the leading tank-killer of the 249th Assault Gun Brigade, during the final defence of Berlin during April 1945. The brigade had distinguished itself on 24 April 1945 by being the only German formation to break into Berlin through the Soviet encircling ring to reinforce the defenders of the capital. Desperately short of ammunition, however, the brigade commander dispatched the reliable Schmidt to the Alkett armaments factory at Spandau where he hoped to find munitions. On his way, however, an SS *Feldjäger* patrol detained Schmidt. In his haste, the brigade commander had dispensed with the formality of written orders (after all, what he was doing – purloining munitions – was illegal) and the SS troopers did not believe Schmidt's story. No doubt they had heard dozens of similar tales about supposed 'special missions' from deserters. The *Feldjäger* quickly convened a drumhead court martial in which the SS *Hauptmann* (Captain) sitting as judge and jury condemned Schmidt to death. The unfortunate soldier was then immediately hanged from the nearest tree.

Such actions undertaken 'pour encourager les autres' undoubtedly stiffened German combat resolve and kept many troops fighting long after any hope of victory had evaporated.

Ideological indoctrination

The German military increasingly attempted to instil a National Socialist world view in its troops as the war progressed in order to buttress further their combat resolve. At the start of the war, indoctrination remained an entirely haphazard and unregulated affair, reflecting the long struggle between the Nazi party and the army to politicise its soldiery. Throughout the early war years, ideological indoctrination was styled 'spiritual strengthening', and was left to unit

Below: An instructor comments on the marksmanship of a students on a shooting exercise. Note the early pattern helmet of the student.

commanders and the euphemistically termed 'welfare officers'. As the war turned against Germany, however, the military increasingly resorted to ideological indoctrination to instil tenacious resistance. But it was not until late 1943 that ideological indoctrination was regularised with the appointment of National Socialist Leadership Officers. These were decorated, veteran leaders who had demonstrated both their battlefield prowess and their commitment to National Socialism. In conjunction with commanding officers, Leadership Officers oversaw the spiritual strengthening of their troops.

Colonel Günther Keil, the commander of the 919th Grenadier Regiment, the last German unit to capitulate to American forces in the Cotentin peninsula in Normandy during late June 1944, exemplified the many senior officers who were prepared to utilise every resource and every opportunity to buttress the morale of their troops. Colonel Keil bragged to his American captors how he and his subordinates had incessantly lectured their troops, whether in the mess

hall, while travelling to and from exercises, or on the parade ground. The ideological indoctrination that Colonel Keil and thousands of other German officers enthusiastically embraced expounded on traditional Nazi themes. It stressed the racial superiority of the German *Volk*, and that the German people faced a Darwinian struggle for national and racial survival in which only the fittest race would survive. Propaganda depicted Nazism as religion and the Führer as God. Simultaneously, increased ideological indoctrination inculcated a sense of superiority, whether with regard to their weapons, cohesion, or training, all in order to buttress troop resolve.

Ideological indoctrination and propaganda contributed directly to German military cohesion and fighting power. Nazi propaganda persuaded many German soldiers that the Allies would not take prisoners. German officers deliberately kept their troops ignorant of the true situation at the front and dealt severely with symptoms of defeatism and anti-Nazi sentiments. Simultaneously, propaganda about powerful new 'vengeance weapons' like the V1 rocket sustained German morale during the last hopeless years of war. Indoctrination helped inculcate *Osthärte* (Eastern hardness), the brutal, savage practices that became the norm in the bitter struggle against the Soviet Union. Such 'hardness' conditioned troops against the terrible conditions in which they fought in the conflict's latter stages.

Illustrative of the efficacy of such propaganda was the amazement that *Obergefreiter* (Corporal) Fritz Dehner of the 272nd Infantry Division felt on being taken prisoner by Canadian troops near Carpiquet airfield west of Caen on 7 July 1944. Though he had long believed the war to be lost, he told his captives, he had continued to fight because he had believed the barrage of propaganda directed at him that asserted that the Western Allies would not take prisoners. A survivor of a previous tour of duty on the Eastern Front, Dehner could not believe the correct handling he received from the Canadians in strict accordance with the Geneva Convention. 'I was not even beaten,' he exulted in the diary he kept during his captivity.

Above: Presenting the colours at a German Army parade during the late 1930s. Rituals such as these gave units a sense of duty and honour.

Contemporary Allied prisoner examinations concluded that most German soldiers remained ideologically committed to Nazism, that they rarely blamed Hitler for German defeats, and that they still believed in ultimate German victory. Nazi ideological indoctrination fortified the will of German soldiers to continue an increasingly hopeless conflict.

Awards and medals

Like all armies, the German Army rewarded battlefield heroism with a variety of awards and medals. This was very important for, as Napoleon once said, 'it is with coloured ribbons that men are led'. Most of the important medals, of course, went to senior officers, though there were a few awards ordinary grenadiers could win. Among these were campaign shields worn usually on the left sleeve or in the form of a cuff band. These were awarded for service in particularly important theatres and campaigns, such as the Narvik Shield for those who fought in the bitter struggle for the Norwegian port in April 1940, or the Kuban Shield for those who fought in the protracted defence of the Kuban bridgehead during the first eight months of 1943. Other obtainable awards included wound badges and close-combat tank destruction medals, awarded to soldiers who individually destroyed an enemy tank in close combat. For outstanding heroism, an ordinary soldier might also gain a coveted Iron Cross, Second Class. Further actions of special bravery could be rewarded by the Iron Cross, First Class, and thereafter by the five ascending classes of the Knight's Cross of the Iron Cross: the Knight's Cross with Oak Leaves, Swords, Diamonds and finally Golden Oak Leaves. During the war, some 2.3 million Iron Crosses, Second Class were issued (about one man in eight received one), 300,000 Iron Crosses, First Class (about one soldier in 60), 5000 Knight's Crosses (about one in 3000 received this award), 871 Oak Leaves, 148 Swords, 13 Diamonds and a solitary Golden Oak Leaves.

That these decorations were cumulative created a powerful incentive for repeated deeds of bravery and heroism. Actions that qualified for a decoration varied between enlisted personnel and officers: more was expected of officers. It hardly needs repeating that eligibility requirements were very stringent. Mere bravery was insufficient: it had to be matched with repeated instances of individual action and initiative. Thus, for example, when Field Marshal Ferdinand Schörner was asked to endorse one Lieutenant-Colonel Mokros for the Oak Leaves of the Knight's Cross for personally leading his regiment in a counter-attack with a machine gun in hand, he demurred, arguing that the officer's actions had been 'a self evident duty' for a commander, rather than an act of exceptional heroism worthy of reward.

The performance of Remi Schrijnen, who gained a reputation as a formidable anti-tank gunner, proved typical of the independent action

Right: A German soldier is greeted enthusiastically by a group of civilians and a solitary member of the Reich Labour Service whilst on manoeuvres sometime before the outbreak of war in 1939. Ordinary Germans were taught to look up to soldiers, and it was considered an honour to be a member of the armed forces by many Germans before the outbreak of war. The private is dressed in the standard Wehrmacht (German Army) field grey uniform. Flowers are wrapped round the two Karabinier 98K rifles in front of him. Note the band just above his helmet brim, used for securing items of foliage to his helmet for camouflage. The photograph has probably been posed for the camera.

combined with exceptional valour required for an award of the Knight's Cross. On 3 March 1944 Schrijnen was wounded for the seventh time and his entire gun crew killed. Yet he refused all entreaties by medical staff to go to a field hospital for adequate treatment. Instead Schrijnen insisted both on being patched up at a forward aid post – however rudimentary the treatment – and on remaining with his unit. His commanding officer assigned him to light duty and forbade Schrijnen from approaching the front line while he convalesced. But when a crisis developed

three days later, he set out for the front in disobedience of his superior's orders and single-handedly manned a still-intact gun. He waged an apparently hopeless battle against an entire battalion of Soviet armour, including a number of the new heavy Josef Stalin II tanks. Schrijnen single-handedly destroyed 11 enemy tanks, including three JS-II vehicles, before being seriously wounded. A relief force found him unconscious and close to death the next day when a counter-attack reoccupied the battery position. Though he had disobeyed his superior, his com-

mander recommended him for the Knight's Cross, for Shrijnen had demonstrated the requisite individual heroism combined with individual initiative, in this case by disobeying orders to save the day, required to receive a Knight's Cross.

Leave

Throughout the war the German Armed Forces adhered to a generous leave policy for its troops, theoretically without distinction as to rank or seniority. Every member of the armed forces was entitled to 14 days' annual leave. In addition,

Above: A German cavalry unit lines up in parade-ground order, ready for inspection. Most cavalry units had been mechanised by 1940.

some were willing to go back and a few even returned early! It is one of the strange phenomena of war that civilians find hard to understand: the longing of service personnel on leave to return to the familiarity of their unit. Some soldiers found it hard, if not impossible, to readjust to civilian attitudes and life at home. Indeed, this environment had become so alien for many troops that they viewed their regiment as their real home. Adolf Strauch, a rifleman in the 2nd Parachute Regiment, typified such sentiments. He confessed in his diary that he spent his entire leave in March 1943 longing to return to the comradeship of his 8th Company based at Mourmelon, France. He found himself unable to relate to his family and peacetime friends and the essentially civilian existence they maintained. He admitted that there was a gulf that separated him from his former friends that he could not bridge. It was, he recorded, thus with joy, rather than sadness, that he returned to his regiment in France.

Support services

Critical to maintaining troop morale and fighting resolve was adequate logistical and support services. Troops, for example, regularly required new clothes, but given the enormous supply needs of the troops, new clothes were a luxury that only arrived periodically after more essential supply requirements had been met. In the 12th Infantry Division, for example, troops received on average a new pair of socks every two months, a change of underwear and a new shirt every six months, and a new uniform just once a year. Consequently, uniforms disintegrated in the field and, after heavy combat, many troops looked more like gypsies than soldiers. Fritz Knappe of the 24th Artillery Regiment could never forget the lice that soon came to share the dirty uniforms of troops in the field. Indelibly etched in his memory was the constant burning in his armpits where the lice gathered for warmth and the incessant scratching that exacerbated rather than alleviated the misery of being infested.

troops might qualify for additional discretionary special leave of up to 21 days for convalescence or a death in the family. Thus at any one time approximately 10 per cent of the German Army was on furlough back home. Unlike British and American soldiers, who often went years before seeing families, the average German soldier could expect to get home at least once a year. It was a rare German soldier indeed who had not been furloughed in two years and such troops received priority on the leave quotas. Commanders also gave priority status to front-line combat troops and to married men with families. This generous leave policy was designed to maintain troop morale and combat effectiveness by reducing personal distractions brought about by extended absence from loved ones and family.

Personnel on leave, however, remained subject to immediate recall on pain of death. However,

Another crucial element in maintaining good morale was the regular receipt of mail. The

German Field Post strenuously endeavoured to ensure that mail from home was delivered to the troops for free. Generally a letter from Germany reached a soldier at the front in under two weeks. Field Postmasters routinely sampled troop letters to evaluate troop morale at the front. Discussion of military matters was censored in sampled mail, but only a fraction of mail could ever be examined. Soldiers were forbidden from sending war souvenirs home, again for very good reasons. In the autumn of 1941, for example, a certain *Gefreiter* (Corporal) Schmidt sent some 'liberated' Soviet munitions home to his younger brother, but they exploded en route, destroying an entire wagon of mail! Schmidt was punished for his indiscretion, but in general it was rare for a soldier to be held accountable for negative comments about either the war or the Nazi leadership (of which there were many). Apart from in enemy action, relatively little of the mail for the

Below: Training to use a 5cm leGW light mortar before the war. Mortars like these gave the infantry added firepower in combat.

troops was ever lost. A sense of the scale of the field post system can be gauged from the statistics of the Eighteenth Army before Leningrad: during the last five months of 1942, its 150,000 troops received a total of 3.5 million mail items.

'Recreation'

From long experience, the German Army had developed a pragmatic attitude toward sex in the military. The army recognised that most soldiers, away from wives and girlfriends, needed sex as a release from the stresses of combat. The relative dearth of women in the typical combat soldier's life also inevitably tended to promote homosexuality which the army strenuously sought to eradicate because it believed such activity to be both morally corrupting and (more importantly) deleterious to good military order. German Military Law banned homosexual acts and those convicted of such 'sex crimes' were subject to harsh punishment, including transfer to a penal unit. There again, those with the right connections could avoid such unpleasantness. Oskar Dirlewanger, a convicted sex offender who was

thrown out of the army, used his political connections to join the *Waffen-SS* and, by 1944, to rise to command the infamous Dirlewanger Brigade, an unsavoury bunch of political prisoners, common convicts and brutal degenerates.

At the same time, the army clearly had to protect soldiers against the dangers of venereal disease which were all too common where soldiers, prostitutes, and camp followers intermixed.

The solution was to establish military brothels where prostitutes could be regulated and frequently checked for disease. There was, however, no official army policy on brothels: they were established purely at the local command level. Obviously commanders' attitudes varied: progressive or perhaps just realistic officers supported them or viewed them as a necessary evil, while others considered brothels to be morally

repugnant and did everything possible to discourage their use by their men.

Parachute Captain Oskar Doll of the 7th Airborne Division exemplified this latter attitude. While he could not forbid his troops from frequenting brothels – to do so might have provoked a mutiny – he nevertheless made it as difficult as possible for them to visit houses of ill-repute. Thus he invariably chose billets as far as

Left: A platoon of steel-helmeted German infantry march through a German square. This parade was held on 29 January 1943 to celebrate the tenth anniversary of Hitler's appointment as Chancellor of Germany in January 1933. Although technically Nazi Germany was near its peak in terms of power and conquered territory, by this stage of the war the tide of the war had begun to turn against Germany, although this would not become apparent until the campaigns of the summer. The decline in Germany's fortunes during the war was not due to the soldiers of the Wehrmacht, *but to the poor utilisation of Germany's factories and resources and Hitler's decision to invade the Soviet Union, thereby over-stretching Germany's armed forces.*

way as possible from the official brothels. He also insisted that those who sought a green ticket to the brothel (access was forbidden without the appropriate pass) dress in full combat gear, complete a 'passing out' inspection before leaving, and then march on foot to and from the brothel in full combat gear. These obstacles succeeded in dissuading all but the most ardent soldiers.

Efforts to regulate sex in order to prevent sexually transmitted diseases were not always successful. On 5 January 1943, for example, some 244 soldiers of the SS *Panzergrenadier* Division *Leibstandarte Adolf Hitler* – then stationed in France – were officially listed as unfit for duty because they had contracted gonorrhoea. Of course, official statistics (of which the Germans were so fond) tended to understate the true extent of the problem. For as long as the soldier was fit, his predicament usually went unreported. The slightly tipsy commander of the *Leibstandarte*, *SS-Oberstgruppenführer* (Colonel-General) Josef 'Sepp' Dietrich, once indiscreetly confided to his boss, the puritanical *Reichsführer-SS* Heinrich Himmler, that a full third of his 20,000-man division had venereal disease. The horrified *Reichsführer-SS* immediately initiated measures designed to crack down on this problem, but the result, like many of his endeavours, met with little success.

For Paul Kammberger and the other young volunteers of the SS *Hitlerjugend* Division, such sexual licence was denied them, since Himmler viewed them as too young and innocent, and wished to avoid the complaints of irate mothers that their young sons had been morally ruined. These teenage SS soldiers were also denied the standard cigarette ration on similar grounds and instead received *in lieu* a boiled sweet ration! What the precise ratio of green passes and cigarettes to boiled sweets was remains a mystery.

Through common experiences of rigorous basic training, iron discipline, constant propaganda, decorations for exemplary performance, generous leave, regular mail, and access to other distractions, the German Army moulded its troops into one of the most formidable war machines the world has ever seen.

Infantry

Despite the more prominent image of panzer divisions or Stuka squadrons as the spearheads of Nazi military power, the traditional but indispensable *Landser* (infantryman) remained the predominant part of Hitler's army throughout the war. The *Landser* may not have represented the cutting edge of technology, but he was the muscle and sinew that provided the essential strength and staying power of Hitler's war machine. Even in mechanised warfare, practically every major battle still came down ultimately to a struggle of man versus man in foxholes, ruined buildings, and shattered woods, in a desperate contest to occupy or defend vital ground.

German infantry fought with impressive tenacity and effectiveness throughout World War II, even after their units had sustained extreme losses. Statistical analyses have concluded that German troops typically inflicted 50 per cent greater casualties on their opponents than they suffered in return, regardless of whether they were attacking or defending, even in the face of overwhelming Allied numerical advantages and air superiority later in the war. One of the most basic elements of this phenomenal military fighting power was unit cohesion: the ability of German soldiers to stick together and to continue operating as an integrated team despite devastating losses, long after the point where other forces would have dissolved into a mass of individuals driven by panic and the mere instinct of self-preservation. German soldiers also showed a remarkable capacity to regroup and form *ad hoc* battle groups composed of stragglers and survivors of various units.

Left: A German infantry section operate their tripod-mounted MG 34 machine gun which is fitted with a special optical sight for sustained fire.

The German infantry came from diverse social, economic, and professional backgrounds. Whereas most other armies tended to allocate manpower primarily according to class, education, or aptitude, the Germans emphasised psychological traits. Personnel officers sought to evaluate each recruit's entire personality, including spiritual qualities and emotional attitudes, not just objective abilities. Particularly sought after was *Einsatzbereitschaft* (a sense of resolution and presence of mind, or a readiness to apply one's entire will to a certain act). Alfred Wessel recalled one such test where he and his fellow recruits were purposely led through a labyrinth of rooms, corridors, and lifts in order to disorient them, then into a dark, windowless cellar, where they had to answer a sudden barrage of unexpected questions. The interrogators, it turned out, were less interested in their answers than in how the recruits reacted under stress. The German Army deemed such qualities no less essential to the infantry than to the other arms, particularly with respect to officer candidates. Thus, the typical *Landser* by no means represented the 'dregs' of German manpower, although by the war's latter stages the Germans were indeed scraping the bottom of the barrel.

Personal qualities would have counted for little, however, if not for the rigorous and relentless training imposed by the *Wehrmacht*. For the infantry recruit, the process began with 16 weeks of basic training (later reduced to eight, as Germany's situation became increasingly desperate). One of the German Army's most familiar mottoes was 'Sweat saves blood.' Guy Sajer learned the significance of this saying when he arrived at Chemnitz barracks in July 1942. In the months that followed, he and his fellow recruits endured countless drills and exercises designed to inflict exhaustion, so-called 'hardness training'. On one occasion, for example, Sajer and his compatriots received no rations for more than 24 hours, during which they had to march and perform manoeuvres that left them cold, wet, and thoroughly miserable. Sajer, however, recognised the higher purpose that distinguished such a regimen from mere petty sadism. Sajer recalled the

Right: An infantry and machine gun section cross the River Bug on 23 September 1939, during the Polish campaign. The horses for the wagons swim alongside the raft built from two dinghies. The speedy advance of the panzer divisions during the campaign often left the infantry lagging behind, a common problem in the early German campaigns of the war. Contrary to the belief of many, the German Army was extremely reliant on horses to provide motive power throughout the war. Although some units were motorised, infantrymen were by and large required to march over most of the territories conquered in 1939–42. This inevitably led to delays in the offensive while panzers waited for their supporting infantry to catch up with them.

drill sergeant as 'a man with a clear idea of a job to be done' who made his recruits realise that if they could not stand a little cold and some vague danger, they would never survive at the front. Nor did such hardships cease at the end of basic training. Infantry *Leutnant* (Lieutenant) Hans Werner Woltersdorf imposed arduous exercises on the men of his unit in occupied France. Although Woltersdorf realised that his men cursed him every time he made them dig holes,

he always made it clear that his purpose was not punishment, but rather a form of 'life insurance'.

Dangerous training

Advanced training added real danger to mere hardship. Guy Sajer recalled an anti-tank exercise where his unit had to take cover in shallow slit trenches and remain there while a platoon of Mark III Panzers drove directly over them. Immediately after the tanks had passed, the

Landsers then had to scramble after them and fix magnetic anti-tank mines to weak spots, such as the joint between hull and turret. Although Sajer did not mention any accidents in this particular drill, one can easily imagine the hazards to life and limb when running alongside and climbing on to a moving tank. Sajer did comment, however, on how dangerous the Panzerfaust anti-tank rocket was, even in training, with its powerful back-blast. In the course of only three weeks of

Above: A German infantry section prepare to attack Soviet positions in the Ukraine. Note the helmet fittings for attaching camouflage.

live-fire drills with the weapon, Sajer's company of 150 men lost four dead and 20 wounded.

It is impossible to calculate precisely how many lives such training later saved in actual combat, but clearly the benefits were significant. Gustav Knickrehm later concluded that the German soldier's main advantage was his 'monstrous training' which inculcated him to carry out 'all orders automatically'. Although, Knickrehm acknowledged, the *Landser* thought about his home and loved ones, he nevertheless 'stood erect and shot' and 'acted automatically as a soldier'. This inculcation helped to preserve the soldier's life: only an idiot would deny this, Knickrehm asserted. After enduring such trials, it is little wonder that *Landsers* developed such strong bonds of comradeship. Indeed, German companies often took on the character of an extended

family. Karl Fuchs suggested as much when he wrote in a letter to his parents that he had become such an integral part of his company that he doubted his ability to leave it ever again. The commanding officer became a father figure, as was expressed by Hans Werner Woltersdorf when he reminisced, 'My unit was my home, my family, which I had to protect.' Rounding out the analogy to family life was the unit's senior NCO or warrant officer, traditionally called the *Spiess*, but often also known as 'Mother'. In the German Army, his role had more to do with morale than discipline, and he routinely acted as an intermediary to convey grievances up the chain of command and generally promote the men's welfare.

Ultimately, of course, discipline also played a critical role in holding the infantry together. Guy Sajer described a hut called the 'dog house' where men were punished by being chained to a wooden beam with hands behind them, and then forced to stand for eight hours and lap their soup from a bowl in this position: all this after a period of 36 continuous hours of hard training. Disciplinary problems, however, remained relatively uncommon, at least until 1945. Soviet commissars might drive their troops like cattle, but German officers knew that combat effectiveness required willing soldiers. The German Army expected its officers to lead by example, and generally they lived up to this ideal. Hans Werner Woltersdorf summed up this 'special leadership principle' as follows: 'The necessary qualification for an officer's career was not the high school diploma but exemplary ability, the true authority. Everyone who led a unit had to be the best man in his unit as well; not the uniform, not being in command, but example made the leader.'

Weapons

Throughout World War II the Mauser Kar 98K bolt-action rifle remained the standard German infantry weapon. Although its virtues included range, accuracy, stopping power, and reliability, Wehrmacht planners realised that most infantry engagements actually took place at close range where a shorter, lighter weapon would suffice. In response, the MP 38/40 'Schmeisser' sub-machine gun had begun to enter service by 1939. Few *Landsers* actually received them until later in the war, but these weapons at least gave special assault units a decided advantage in close combat. The Germans also made extensive use of hand grenades, which offered *Landsers* the priceless advantage of attacking around corners or over parapets without exposing themselves. In World War II the standard German grenades were the egg-shaped Model 39 and the more familiar Model 24 'potato-masher' whose wooden handle afforded greater throwing range.

Ten infantrymen led by an NCO made up a rifle squad, with the addition of an MG 34 light machine gun. The firepower afforded by this weapon, with its belt-fed 7.92mm ammunition and high rate of fire, gave the German infantry one of its most important advantages. Three squads (increased to four between 1939 and 1940) made a rifle platoon, with the addition of a command team and a 5cm mortar. A rifle company consisted of three platoons plus a headquarters squad and a heavy machine gun section. An infantry battalion included three rifle companies, a headquarters company, and a heavy weapons company, the latter fielding six heavy machine guns and six 8.1cm mortars. Three battalions composed a regiment, with the addition of the regimental headquarters, an infantry howitzer company, and an anti-tank company.

The German infantry did have significant shortcomings, however. The rapid expansion of the army after 1933 considerably diluted the quality of the elite *Reichswehr* (the small professional army of the Weimar period), with serious shortages of both officers and NCOs, who meanwhile struggled to train masses of new draftees. Transport remained distinctly old-fashioned, with a profusion of over 2000 horses and relatively few motor vehicles in each division. Equipment shortages also plagued many German units, which often received older weapons – such as the 1908-vintage MG 08 water-cooled machine gun – or else made do with captured foreign equipment.

Overall, the German infantry nevertheless entered World War II better prepared than any of

their opponents. Yet no one could be certain of the outcome when Hitler again plunged the nation into a war on two fronts. Klaus von Bismarck (a descendant of the famous Chancellor) was a young infantry officer in 1939. He later wrote that his comrades were neither exactly ecstatic about the war, nor did they really believe the propaganda they heard. All the same, he admitted, 'we were all captivated by the situation. We were highly impressed with ourselves – our vitality, our strength, and our discipline.'

Although the Germans won a crushing victory in Poland, the campaign revealed a serious flaw in their lack of training for night engagements. Recognising such shortcomings and taking steps to correct them, even after such a resounding victory, was one of the hallmarks of German military effectiveness. Considering the real hard-

Below: German signal troops on a training exercise lay out a field telephone line, used for secure communications on the battlefield.

ships involved in realistic night training, particularly the effects of sleep deprivation, it is not so difficult to understand why even the Germans had tended to neglect them previously. But after Poland, they bit the bullet. Hans Werner Woltersdorf recalled the despairing looks he received from his men when they learned that they must assemble for night manoeuvres after a full day of normal training. 'At sunrise they stood there again, covered in dust, filthy, and wanting nothing more eagerly than to be able to hit the hay now. But it wasn't to be! Two hours later, weapon and gun roll call, because weapon care and constant readiness for action are essential!'

Mountain troops

Mountain infantry troops (*Gebirgsjäger*) played a key role in the spring 1940 German invasion of Norway. Experts in skiing and climbing, these troops came primarily from the Alpine regions of Austria and Bavaria. Slipping past the British blockade, German warships carried lightly equipped elements of the 2nd and 3rd Mountain Divisions to seize Trondheim and Narvik, which they had to hold until relieved by additional forces advancing northward from Oslo. The Germans had to break through a succession of blocking positions held by ad hoc Norwegian forces, which were attempting to buy time for the arrival of Allied reinforcements. In a number of such engagements, the Germans found to their dismay that the Norwegian infantry generally were better marksmen. However, losses to snipers did not prevent the Germans from linking up with their comrades to the north: in most respects the German infantry proved decisively superior to the ill-trained Norwegians and British Territorials.

In the May–June 1940 German onslaught in the West, once the panzer divisions had driven through to the Channel coast and forced the northern Allied armies to evacuate or surrender at Dunkirk, the brunt of the fighting in the final phase of the campaign fell once again on the German infantry. By this time, in fact, the panzer divisions had suffered such heavy losses (due to breakdowns as well as enemy action) that

Above: A German machine gun crew carry their 7.92mm MG 34, with extra belts of ammunition slung over the gunner's shoulders.

there was no possibility of another lightning thrust to destroy the remaining French forces around Paris. Instead, German infantry divisions conducted a more deliberate but no less impressive offensive that demolished any remaining Allied hopes of holding the capital, leaving

France with little choice but to sue for peace. Thus, the 1939–40 campaigns proved not only the dazzling new power of mechanised operations, but also the essential prowess of the German *Landser*. In such heady days of victory, few could imagine what lay ahead.

After several months' lull during late 1940 and early 1941, German infantry went into action again to spearhead Operation 'Marita', the April 1941 Axis invasion of Yugoslavia and Greece.

Mountain troops were essential to this campaign, given the difficult topography of the region. Alois Redl described how a small detachment of his battalion infiltrated the Yugoslav defences around a bridge near Belgrade by paddling across the treacherous Mur River. Although spotted before reaching the far bank, the *Jägers* managed to reach it, defused demolition charges on the bridge, and successfully stormed a bunker to clear the way for their comrades. The

Above: Close up of a bearded German soldier by some form of vision device. Scopes like this one were used on rangefinders and aiming devices.

Oberfeldwebel (NCO) who commanded the assault received the Knight's Cross.

The swiftness of Yugoslavia's collapse gave little indication of how difficult it would be to hold the region as Tito's partisan forces gathered strength. In Greece, however, the Germans faced a determined and well-entrenched foe from the outset. After one assault, the exhausted *Jägers* paused to regroup. 'My life nearly ended at that point,' one of them recalled. 'From out of nowhere, or so it seemed, a company of Greek infantry came charging at us with bayonets fixed. It was an absolutely frightening experience as the enemy charged down the slope towards us.' At the last possible moment, the Germans recovered from their shock and shredded the counter-attack with a hail of machine gun fire. 'We killed all the enemy soldiers before they could reach us with their bayonets and fight us hand to hand,' the

veteran concluded. In general, German infantry seemed less inclined to seek hand-to-hand combat than some of their opponents such as the Greeks, or the Gurkhas with their kukri knives.

Barbarossa

The 1940–41 battles in the Balkans and North Africa soon became a mere sideshow, however, in relation to the scale and unrestrained savagery of the Eastern Front, where the great majority of German soldiers would fight and die. Alfred Opitz recalled that as he and his fellow soldiers lay in their forward positions in Poland on the night of 21 June 1941, the air itself 'smelled of something enormous'. Another *Landser*, Friedrich Grupe, wrote, '3:00 a.m. Helmets are put on, rifles loaded ... Now the earth rumbles and shakes, before us flashes the glow of fires ... The time of the infantryman is here. We race forward.' This was the beginning of Operation 'Barbarossa', Hitler's massive invasion of the Soviet Union, involving 3.3 million Axis troops, most of whom were infantry. Infantry divisions received additional horses to help sustain the advance, but the bulk of the army still had to travel by foot. The advancing troops soon found that Russia would be far different from their earlier campaigns. The immense distances they had to cover defied imagination. A German war correspondent wrote that when a German infantryman spoke of his experiences in Soviet Russia, the first thing he said was that despite the country being flat, all 'the roads go up hill irrespective of the direction in which they run'. The journalist added that the German soldiers' 'greatest efforts' were not made during battle, even though these troops knew they had to fight hard; rather, the *Landsers* had to expend 'tremendous spiritual effort' just to overcome the vast distances involved. Guy Sajer observed that the word 'exhaustion' had 'nothing to do with the "exhaustion" I've encountered since the war' on the Eastern Front, which could 'strip a strong man of 15 pounds of weight in a few days'.

Primitive living conditions and lack of supplies were among the most universal experiences of *Landsers* in Russia. Even when not on the march, petty miseries such as lice could make routine existence almost unbearable. Holding a relatively quiet sector in the Crimea in May 1942, Alois Dwenger wrote, 'I believe that true heroism lies in bearing this dreadful everyday life.' Such discomforts are of course an infantryman's lot in almost any time and place, but the Russian winter was unique. German uniforms and equipment proved inadequate, to say the least, and frostbite proved extremely common. *Landsers* survived by expedients such as woven straw overshoes which were warm but extremely bulky, and makeshift camouflage smocks fashioned from bedsheets. Another common improvisation among infantrymen was a handmade snowshoe-like base for light machine guns, to prevent the bipod from sinking into the snow.

Below: The Machinenpistole *MP38, seen here being fired by a paratroop at Cassino, was one of the main German infantry weapons of the war.*

'When will spring finally come?' wrote one young officer in his journal. 'At night it is icy cold in this wretched region. We struggle to get into the ground.' Another officer recalled his men's horror on finding that their machine guns had jammed from the cold, leaving them virtually defenceless, until someone discovered that they could defrost the weapons by rubbing petrol on them.

The Soviets seemed to have no regard for losses and their manpower reserves appeared unlimited. Writing in his journal directly afterward, Leopold von Thadden-Trieglaff described a night assault on his unit's position in March 1943: 'The cries of "Hurrah" from almost all sides by the attacking Russians; shouts, screams ... withering fire ... We dished it out to the mass of Russians who had penetrated the position on my right ... answered their cries of "Hurrah" with mocking shouts ... We stood like oaks with the consciousness of impending death.' Overrun on both flanks, the encircled Germans held fast until

daylight when a relief column arrived. Yet the ordeal had taken its toll: 'I was so shaken that I almost cried,' he confessed, before adding, 'When might this hideous defensive struggle come to an end?' With bitter irony, Thadden-Trieglaff got his answer the next day when he was killed.

Never was infantry combat more intense than at Stalingrad, where the Soviets eventually destroyed the entire German Sixth Army and turned the tide of the war during the winter of 1942–43. A German lieutenant wrote of 15 days' continuous fighting over the ruins of a single house, filled with explosions, smoke, blood, and body fragments. 'Stalingrad,' he concluded, 'is no longer a town. By day it is an enormous cloud of burning, blinding smoke; it is a vast furnace lit by the reflection of the flames. And when night arrives, one of those scorching, howling, bleeding nights, the dogs plunge into the Volga and swim desperately to gain the other bank.' The officer's

Below: A decorated anti-tank gunner inspects the penetration hole one of his rounds has made in the side armour of a Russian armoured vehicle.

closing comment in his diary was that 'Animals flee this hell ... only men endure.'

News of the desperate fighting in Stalingrad caused another *Landser*, Harry Mielert, to reflect on the psychological effect of ammunition shortages. 'They are defending themselves with entrenching spades and rifle butts,' he wrote. 'When a soldier has no more ammunition he is lonely. Ammunition ... gives him confidence and security; it also has a metaphysical impact on his heart. The other is like the struggle between wild animals.' In addition to the savage determination of Soviet resistance, Russian weaponry proved a nasty shock to the invaders. One example was the crude but effective PPSh sub-machine gun, which the Russians produced in massive numbers. Although the MP 38/40 was a good match, most *Landsers* still carried rifles and were often unnerved by the firepower of entire Russian units with sub-machine guns. Many Germans began using captured Soviet guns as a stop-gap.

The Germans did succeed in mass-producing an excellent new light machine gun, the famous MG 42, which gave the *Landsers* a crucial edge in

firepower. Though similar to the MG 34, the new design made it simpler to change barrels when they began to overheat. With a very high cyclic rate of fire of up to 1500 rounds per minute, the MG 42 sounded more like tearing fabric than the 'tap-tap-tap' of other machine guns.

Soviet tanks

Even more than sub-machine guns, Soviet tanks presented a terrible shock to the German infantry. Between 1941 and 1942, the T34 and KV1 proved almost impervious to German weapons such as the standard 37mm anti-tank gun or the obsolescent Model 39 anti-tank rifle. Prior to 'Barbarossa', German infantry seldom had faced enemy armour on their own, but the experience soon became all too familiar. Writing to his wife, Harry Mielert described an 'awful' delaying action where he and four other men tried to hold a position against a night assault by five Soviet tanks carrying infantry on their decks. 'At close range we fought the infantry,' he wrote, 'but the threatening steel colossi roared on past us, shooting from all barrels.' At last came a green star-shell, the signal to withdraw. 'Now began a race for our lives. The tanks pursued us over two kilometres, constantly firing and blocking the way.' Eventually only Mielert and one other rifleman made it back to friendly lines. Two months later, Mielert wrote again of being 'hunted as one would only hunt a wounded animal', and having 'sat five hours in a swamp, in ice cold water up to my stomach, under continuous fire from a tank'. Two weeks later he was dead.

New weapons and tactics provided some counter-measures such as anti-tank mines and shaped-charge grenades, and eventually the potent Panzerschreck and Panzerfaust rocket-launchers. Special training could help, but nothing could prepare soldiers entirely for the shattering experience of facing enemy armour with little more than bare flesh and raw courage. Scoring a kill required incredible luck as well as nerves of steel. In the battle for Moscow, Hans Werner Woltersdorf received a bizarre surprise when he climbed on to the deck of a Soviet tank and attempted to drop a grenade down the turret,

only to find that the hatch was secured by a padlock, apparently to prevent the crew from escaping. He finally destroyed the tank by firing a signal flare in through a smaller opening.

An anonymous *Landser* described another hair-raising encounter with a T34. As it passed close by his foxhole, he clambered out and attempted to fix a magnetic anti-tank grenade to the hull, only to discover that the tank was covered with a form of concrete to prevent grenades from sticking. Suddenly the tank crew spotted him, spun the vehicle, and attempted to run him over. Falling into a shallow trench, the *Landser* managed to stick the grenade to the unprotected belly of the tank as it passed over him. Moments later the grenade exploded, destroying the tank. 'I was alive and the Russians were dead,' he concluded. 'I was trembling in every limb.'

Severe and irreplaceable losses in Russia and Tunisia prompted a general reorganisation of German infantry divisions in October 1943. Regiments were reduced from three to only two battalions, and platoons were reduced from four squads to only three. In early 1944, further changes reduced the size of a squad to only nine men. The net effects of such reshuffling produced enough new infantry units to patch up the lines in Russia and Italy for a few months, but they also made it clear to *Landsers* throughout the army that Germany was in serious trouble.

As enemy pressure increased on all fronts, German infantrymen also felt the effects of strain on the supply system. One mundane but discouraging sign was the declining quality of uniforms. The older Pattern 1936 tunic, webbing, and jackboots gave way to new types by 1943, designed to conserve scarce materials. Canvas belts replaced leather, synthetic fibres increasingly replaced wool, and cloth anklets supplemented low-topped boots. Even the distinctive German coalscuttle helmet changed shape slightly in 1943, saving a bit of steel by reducing the curvature of the forward rim. *Landsers* almost invariably preferred the old equipment and tried to make the better stuff last as long as possible.

In early 1944, German infantry units dug in to hold the Channel coast against the impending

Allied invasion. Though discipline remained tight, morale had begun to deteriorate as news of defeats on the Eastern Front and elsewhere filtered through the ranks. Werner Beibst, an 18-year-old *Landser* on the 'Atlantic Wall' fortifications, later wrote of his 'impression that many people thought the war was not going well for Germany, although we certainly never discussed it; one simply didn't.' All the same, soldiers found ways of expressing themselves. Beibst's unit received special briefings on how to

react to enemy commando raids after several sentries mysteriously disappeared from their bunkers overlooking the beaches at night. After one lecture, the instructor asked a soldier what he would do if commandos appeared suddenly and attempted to take him prisoner. Perfectly deadpan, he replied: 'Well, go with them, of course!' Beibst believed the decline in morale had a lot to do with inferior rations.

By early September 1944 it seemed only a matter of weeks before the advancing Allies must

Left: German Volksturm (Home Guard) militia troops man a slit trench in East Prussia, November 1944, during training. They are armed with the trusty Karabiner 98K rifles – whose 7.92mm bullets were to prove of little use against the approaching Soviet tanks. The old and young alike were called up for service in a last-ditch attempt to repel the Allies from the Reich's own soil. Many Home Guard volunteers, particularly the Hitler Youth members, fought fanatically, but all were ill-trained and poorly-equipped, and in most cases the Home Guard units were of little more than nuisance value against the advancing Allies. By late 1944 the Wehrmacht *was in full retreat on both fronts.*

Battle of the Bulge

The Germans pinned their remaining hopes on one more offensive in December 1944. This, now known as the Battle of the Bulge, was their desperate attempt to divide the western Allied armies and drive through to Antwerp. An NCO in the 167th *Volksgrenadier* Division wrote, 'This is glorious. We are bitterly cold, but it will be warmer on the Channel. God must be with us this time.' Another soldier wrote to his sister that in the hours prior to the assault he was 'full of excitement and expectation of what the next days will bring'. Some of his peers, he confessed, 'believe in living but life is not everything! It is enough to know that we attack and will throw the enemy from the homeland. It is a holy task. Above me is the terrific noise of the V1s and artillery, the voice of war.' The writer almost certainly died shortly thereafter. After some initial success, the offensive foundered.

Still the German infantry fought on, increasingly hopeless, yet determined to stave off the vengeance of the Red Army. Whole divisions ceased to exist, yet local commanders still managed to improvise battle groups by rounding up survivors of other units. In the many rearguard infantry actions of early 1945, 'picked men' who were considered expendable – the old, the very young, or those unable to march – were posted beside a road in a foxhole or trees with a Panzerfaust or machine gun, their orders were simply to kill as many of the pursuing enemy as they could and to retreat no further. Victory was beyond hope, but such sacrifices bought time for thousands of civilians to escape westward.

The perseverance, courage, and skill of the German infantry was a key ingredient of Hitler's military power. In practically every type of terrain and situation, they consistently outfought their opponents, winning such impressive victories in the early years that they began to seem invincible, not only to the enemy, but also to their own leaders. Thus, the *Landser*'s success set the stage for his ultimate demise when the accumulation of strategic blunders and supply shortages created battlefield odds that Germany's armed forces ultimately found insurmountable.

arrive in Berlin. Against all odds, however, the Germans rallied on the borders of the Fatherland. Last-ditch mobilisation produced a final wave of reinforcements, so-called *Volksgrenadier* divisions, which were reduced-establishment infantry formations. Comprised mostly of men over 50 and boys in their mid-teens, *Volksgrenadiers* helped to shore up the Reich's crumbling defences and bought another few months for Hitler's dying regime, but at a terrible human price.

Panzer Forces

The dominant instrument of the German Army during World War II was the panzer (armoured) arm, which spearheaded the bold mobile warfare campaigns of the 1939–42 German *Blitzkrieg* ('Lightning War'). During the 1930s the Germans evolved a new strategic concept of rapidly advancing armoured forces that conducted deep penetrations to paralyse the enemy, and thus destroy their cohesion. In 1935 the German Army formed its first three panzer divisions. Hitler encouraged such developments, since the creation of an offensive military instrument capable of swift and decisive victory suited the Führer's expansionist goals.

The combat effectiveness that German panzer divisions demonstrated throughout World War II owed much to the fact that they constituted well-balanced all-arms formations rather than just a mass of tanks. The 1935 armoured division included, in addition to two regiments of tanks, motorised infantry, artillery, engineers, and signallers, plus anti-tank and reconnaissance troops. In September 1939, a panzer force of six armoured divisions participated in the German invasion of Poland. In campaigns that followed until the final Nazi defeat in May 1945, the soldiers of the panzer divisions spearheaded the offensive and defensive actions undertaken by the German Army.

France 1940

The Germans envisaged their panzer divisions as strategic instruments of high tempo manoeuvre

Left: Trainee tank crews are put through their paces on an early model Panzer IV tank by the NSKK, the panzer crew training organisation.

warfare. A classic example of such employment involved the actions of *Generaloberst* (Colonel-General) Heinz Guderian's XIX Panzer Corps during the May 1940 German invasion of the West. The German attack plan reinforced pre-existing Allied perceptions about the likely axes of German advance with feint attacks in the north plus a threat against the Maginot Line to the south. Instead the German main effort pushed a concentrated armoured thrust of seven panzer divisions (including Guderian's three such formations) through the supposedly impassable – and hence weakly defended – terrain of the Ardennes. On 10 May the Luftwaffe swiftly achieved air superiority and used this to protect the German armour from Allied air attack as it moved swiftly through the Ardennes.

Once through this restrictive terrain, Guderian faced one last obstacle before he reached the open French countryside beyond: the French defences along the southern bank of the River Meuse at Sedan. Guderian's soldiers faced an assault river crossing against prepared enemy defences, a tough mission which left scant room for tactical manoeuvre. Hence, as Panzer III gunner Sergeant Hans Rubelt recalled, the 1st Panzer Division's armour just lined up on the northern side of the river and provided direct fire support for the assault infantry. On 13 May at Sedan, the intimate all-arms cooperation employed by the German panzer divisions proved essential for success. As the 1st Division's Luftwaffe air liaison teams called down Stuka dive-bomber attacks, its assault engineers – like *Gefreiter* (Corporal) Heinz Falley – and infantry paddled feverishly across the river in dinghies under the protection of an intense hail of aerial-, artillery- and tank-fire. Although the assault infantry took heavy casualties in the face of withering French fire, they managed to consolidate a bridgehead on the other side of the river.

During that evening, as several battalions of the 1st Panzer Division's Rifle Brigade crossed the Meuse, the lead German forces continued to expand their bridgehead and seized the vital La Marfée Heights. That night, once engineers had constructed a bridge over the river, the division's

armour, including Rubelt's tank, crossed into the bridgehead south of Sedan. By the morning of 14 May sufficient armour had dug in among the defensive positions held by the infantry that the Germans managed to hold the much-delayed French counter-attack. As the 1st Panzer pushed south, entire French units broke and ran, the first evidence to reach the French High Command that their troops could not withstand the shock action imposed by the German *Blitzkrieg*. Sedan had fallen, and now the central heartland of France lay open to the panzers.

Later that day, despite aerial intelligence of approaching French reinforcements, Guderian took the risk of ordering two of his three divisions to turn west and race swiftly toward the sea. That day, Rubelt recollected, the 1st Panzer Division charged into the interior of France, bypassing any cohesive resistance it met, and continued to advance until its troops had exhausted their last drop of petrol. By the end of the next day, the 1st and 2nd Panzer Divisions had advanced 64km (40 miles) against weakening French resistance. The sheer tempo and paralysis imposed every time German tanks arrived unexpectedly at some French command centre increasingly disintegrated French morale. For example, to the north where two other panzer corps raced to out-do Guderian's advance, *Generalmajor* (Major-General) Erwin Rommel's 7th Panzer Division bagged some 10,000 French prisoners in just two days at the price of just 20 casualties. By 21 June, Guderian's two divisions had punched a hole through the crumbling Allied line and reached the English Channel at Abbeville, cutting off the Allied forces in the north. Here exhausted panzer crews, including Rubelt's, grabbed some sleep before getting down to much needed maintenance on their vehicles, for the rapid advance had taken its toll on many of the German tanks. By early June, the Germans had forced the remaining encircled Allied forces to surrender, although large numbers had managed to escaped to Britain in the 'miracle of Dunkirk'. During late May, however, the Germans had discovered the risks and weaknesses inherent in *Blitzkrieg*. First, on 21 May, a

Above: Heinz Guderian, Germany's leading armoured warfare general, checks on the progress of his forces near the front line.

limited Allied counter-thrust at Arras shook the German High command and prompted Hitler to issue a halt order, which gave the British time to improvise a defensive perimeter around Dunkirk. Second, in the streets of Calais two German armoured divisions suffered heavy casualties in urban combat. These minor setbacks aside, the soldiers of the panzer divisions nevertheless had achieved a stunning success during this campaign with their *Blitzkrieg* techniques.

Mobile defence

Although offensive use of the panzer divisions brought Germany significant military successes prior to 1941, its *Blitzkrieg* failed to conquer the Soviet colossus during the 1941 Axis invasion, code-named Operation 'Barbarossa'. Indeed, after 1942, Red Army offensives increasingly forced

the Germans onto the defensive. In such situations the Germans turned again to their elite panzer divisions, but now to perform a new tactical mission: to spearhead mobile defence. Field Marshal Erich von Manstein's masterful spring 1943 Kharkov counter-stroke constituted an excellent example of such tactics. Disobeying Hitler's orders, the hardened troopers of the newly constituted SS Panzer Corps abandoned their static defence of Kharkov and then joined Manstein's coordinated counter-stroke that smashed into the over-extended spearheads of the Soviet offensive then pushing rapidly through the Ukraine. In appalling conditions, *SS-Sturmann* (Lance Corporal) Heinz Stuss recalled, superior German tank gunnery and all-arms cooperation recaptured Kharkov and flung back the Soviet spearheads, inflicting severe casualties on them. Unfortunately for the Germans, their declining combat capabilities prevented them from repeating such success in the other elastic defence operations which they enacted in the East during the rest of 1943.

Static defence

Increasingly between 1944 and 1945 the Germans abandoned elastic defence as growing troop shortages, lack of fuel, and the rising threat of Allied air superiority hindered German employment of such tactics. Instead, German tactics shifted to a more static defence using field fortifications. By 1944, while German infantry divisions usually held the front, the High Command increasingly found itself forced to commit armour to the front, either to fill gaps in the line or to beef up the combat power of weakened defences. The Germans recognised this as a tactical misuse of their armour, but faced no alternative in the circumstances. In order to construct such field fortifications, German armoured divisions in the East ruthlessly conscripted the local population, irrespective of age or gender, to dig trenches or lay wire obstacles. On 24 July 1943, for example, Private Hans Brandt of the 18th Panzer Division participated in the rounding-up of all available Soviet manpower, older children included, to work on defensive positions.

The actions of the Panzer *Lehr* (Demonstration) Division during the summer 1944 Normandy campaign illustrates how Allied pressure forced the Germans into the tactical misuse of their armour. During the protection from Allied observation provided by the short Norman night of 9–10 June 1944, the Panzer *Lehr* joined the German defensive line north of Caen. The Division's 140 operational tanks deployed in four-vehicle troops, like that of Captain Hans Felmer, in well-camouflaged defensive positions among the copses that littered the Norman Bocage. Each of the division's *panzergrenadier* platoons occupied a stretch of Norman hedgerow between La Belle Epine and Cristot. A troop of four tanks deployed to support each of these platoons. Given the terrible threat posed by Allied tactical air power, camouflaging their vehicles became an imperative and time-consuming task for the tank crews of the Panzer *Lehr*, including that of Felmer's troop. Once his crews meticulously had covered the tank with foliage,

one soldier moved forward toward enemy lines to ascertain if parts of the vehicle remained visible, and then reported back. Felmer's crews had to repeat this process until no part of the tank remained visible to the enemy. The tanks of several other troops, however, sought protection from air attack by taking up position under haystacks or in the few barns that dotted the area. Wherever these positions, all of these crews then faced another boring task if they were to stay alive: the tell-tale marks of flattened ground where the tank had approached its defensive position had to be disguised to prevent air attack. Felmer's tank crews had to spend long, tedious, hours straightening every single piece of bent wheat and covering all the broken foliage to obliterate any evidence of the movement of their vehicles to their new positions.

Below: A mixed column of German vehicles, including two Panzer I light tanks, advance through a wood in Poland.

On that first day of defensive duties, these tank crews – including Felmer's – also had to dig the obligatory slit trench under the vehicle, where the crew slept at night. In addition, many dug another ditch nearby, in case the tank burned and threatened the safety of any crew in the trench below it. Captain Felmer's four crews positioned around La Belle Epine had to endure 14 tense days of this static warfare. Each day the crew spent many long hours observing the British lines, calculating the ranges and bearings of likely enemy routes of advance and re-adjusting the camouflage protection. Most mornings an Allied artillery barrage would erupt around their position, straining all the crew's nerves to breaking point as the inferno raged around their metal boxes. Although Felmer's crews only became involved in four engagements during this fortnight, the tense hours of interminable waiting placed considerable strain on his men. All the German crews sighed with relief when after 14 days, the division redeployed into reserve positions after a new infantry division replaced them at the front. Such experiences became common for panzer soldiers between 1944 and 1945 as Allied pressure forced the Germans to employ their armour in this static defensive manner, a policy which also surrendered any tactical initiative to the Allies.

Withdrawals

After 1942, the Germans increasingly had to employ their armour to conduct holding actions to cover the retreat of less mobile units. Successful implementation of such actions became crucial if the German Army was to extract less mobile units from threatened enemy encirclement. By 1944, the panzer arm had proved itself particularly skilled at such operations. In the West during early September 1944, for example, as the Allies pushed forward rapidly through Belgium, officers such as Colonel Ritgen of the Panzer *Lehr* fought desperate yet effective delaying actions with their meagre armoured battle groups to cover the headlong and disorganised retreat of less mobile German units. Similarly, during withdrawals in the East, the

panzergrenadier regiments within armoured divisions frequently carried out scorched earth policies by destroying everything they left behind to deny any advantage to the enemy. During the retreat to the River Dniepr in autumn 1943, soldiers of the *Grossdeutschland* Division, for example, recalled how their unit expelled at gun point 13,000 terrified Soviets citizens from the villages which the Division abandoned during its withdrawal. Indeed, during April and May 1945, withdrawal operations dominated the actions many Germany armoured divisions undertook as they fell back in chaos in face of the inexorable Allied advance into the Reich itself.

Redeployment

Strategic redeployment between theatres often brought novel experiences for the soldiers of German panzer divisions. Wherever possible, rail transport carried the men and equipment for most of the way during redeployments, with the division moving by road only to and from the nearest railhead at either end of the journey to minimise wear on the tanks' mechanical components. In early 1942, the Panzer 38(t)-equipped reserve panzer battalion – in which Private Henry Metelmann served – redeployed by rail to the Soviet Union from Tours in France. The tank crews first helped local workers load the vehicles on to flat-bed wagons before they themselves clambered aboard two of the three aged wooden carriages at the rear of the train: the third remained reserved for the officers. The two soldiers' carriages were grievously overcrowded, and at night some of the tank crews had to try to sleep in the luggage racks since all the seats and floor had been filled with resting troops.

During its journey across Europe, Metelmann's train stopped on average every 48 hours so that the troops could get some decent hot food from railway canteens rather than their inadequate field rations. Experienced soldiers seized such opportunities to rush forward to the locomotive to gather hot water with which to wash themselves. To pass the time in the candle-lit carriages – no electric power was available – the soldiers read, talked about their families and the war situation, or sang in accompaniment to popular tunes like the *Lorelei* and *Wacht am Rhein* played on mouth organs. After 14 uncomfortable days, the trains reached the frozen wastes of the Ukraine. Here disaster struck: the lavatories froze solid due to the extreme cold. Metelmann recalled with typically black soldier's humour that those men who simply could not wait until the train next stopped had to climb outside the carriage on to the running board and, gripping on for dear life in the freezing wind, squat over the side to do what had to be done!

Training

Squatting over a carriage running board was a technique no German panzer recruit learned during training. Nevertheless, all panzer arm personnel received extensive training to reflect their spearhead role. After recruits had nearly completed their standard infantry basic training, they put themselves forward for selection by the specialist arms. The panzer force, however, only accepted those soldiers who had excelled during this preliminary phase. Panzer arm recruits, like Private Karl Huber, next moved on to specialised instruction at dedicated armoured schools. This training emphasised not just the technical aspects of independent tank warfare, such as fighting tactics, gunnery, ballistics, and maintenance, but also the operation of armour in close cooperation with other combat arms, notably the panzergrenadiers, the anti-tank troops, and the artillery. German tank crews, especially gunners, received substantial training and instruction in the art of gunnery, and honed their skills – even late into the war – through extensive field exercises on armoured training grounds like those at Putlos, northern Germany. The importance of this instruction was reflected in the quality of those who directed the training, who included some of Germany's most experienced and accomplished officers.

As a result of these efforts German tank crews usually achieved a superior standard of gunnery through much of World War II, though this was also aided by the high quality of optical equipment mounted in German tanks. This level of

Right: This view of the 7.5cm-gunned Marder II (Sdkfz 131) self-propelled anti-tank gun illustrates well the tall gun cradle fitted to support the weight of the vehicle's main armament when travelling away from the front line. The Marder II was based on the chassis of the Panzer II tank, which was effectively obsolete by the outbreak of war. The German Army would use a variety of gun platforms throughout the war, using converted older tanks as newer models like the Panther and Tiger tanks became available. The Marder II was a popular addition to the Wehrmacht's armoury, despite its high profile, as it gave the anti-tank units much needed firepower against the Soviet T34 tank.

achievement was exemplified by *SS-Oberscharführer* (Sergeant) Balthasar Woll, Michael Wittmann's gunner, who recorded a personal tally of 81 tank kills on the Eastern Front. An experienced German tank crew operating at typical combat ranges might expect to hit a target on their second or third shots. Of course, though, as the war progressed, the Replacement Army found it ever harder to maintain the quality of replacements sent to the frontline panzer divisions. First, the High Command had to curtail the length of panzer division training to

increase the flow of replacements to the front. Second, the availability of ammunition required for extensive training exercises dwindled as frontline demands absorbed all German production. Indeed, in spring 1945, the High Command mobilised the remaining half-trained armoured recruits, together with their instructors and aged training tanks, and marched them to the front in one final attempt to halt the inexorable Allied advance. Though these improvised units displayed some of the élan characteristic of the early-war German armoured forces, as Private Karl

Fuchs of the *Müncheberg* Panzer Division recalled, they nonetheless soon succumbed to numerically superior Allied forces during the maelstrom that engulfed the Wehrmacht during April and May 1945.

Leisure

During the relatively few periods of rest and refit behind the lines snatched between intense bouts of combat, German panzer crews sought to enjoy their meagre leisure time with sports and social gatherings. When the 101st SS Heavy Tank

Battalion was deployed in Italy during early September 1943, its troops organised a 'night and fog' operation to appropriate a large locally made parmesan cheese. The assault troops used a bayonet to divide up the stolen cheese and then hid their pieces in their tanks until they could be enjoyed at a forthcoming unofficial celebration. Unfortunately the unit commander, panzer ace *SS-Untersturmführer* (Second Lieutenant) Michael Wittmann, heard of the theft and came to inspect his troops' vehicles: to avoid being caught and disciplined, the conspirators had to quickly eat their cheese portion before Wittman reached their vehicle. One *SS-Schütze* (Private) recollected that the ensuing indigestion put off the soldiers' interest in such 'special' operations for several weeks!

Discipline

Despite their elite status, the troops of German panzer divisions experienced the same severe discipline received by the other arms of the Wehrmacht. This became increasingly true on the Eastern Front after 1943, when the High Command strove to keep disillusioned German troops in the field through emphasising the loyalty they owed to their comrades and by threatening them with draconian punishment. When Henry Metelmann, while on exercise in the Crimea during spring 1942, got his Panzer 38(t) stuck in the mud through careless driving, and then back-chatted a superior during an upbraiding, he received a punishment of three days imprisonment in a stable. Far worse, though, was the humiliation that preceded his jail sentence: his commander forced him to wear a triangular paper hat and, with a stick between his legs, gallop up and down in front of the assembled company shouting out that he was a little panzer that had got stuck in the mud.

Between 1944 and 1945, the High Command subjected its panzer troops to ever harsher threats to motivate them given the declining

Left: The crew of a Panzer IV take a break on top of their vehicle. The ripple effect on the armour is caused by Zimmerit anti-magnetic mine paste.

battlefield situation. Roving *Feldjäger* military police patrols combed the rear areas and hanged from the nearest tree any frontline soldiers they found in the area without good cause: pour encourager les autres. During March 1945, for example, *Oberstleutnant* (Lieutenant-Colonel) Hans von Luck of the 21st Panzer Division sent a highly decorated veteran sergeant back on verbal orders to the divisional workshop to bring forward an armoured tractor that had just been repaired. A *Feldjäger* patrol encountered the sergeant and, in the absence of written proof of his mission, promptly executed him in front of the assembled workshop troops. Hans von Luck complained bitterly about the incident to his superiors, but his protests cut little ice. By 1945, in addition to the battlefield horrors panzer soldiers faced, like burning alive trapped in a 'brewing up' tank, they now faced similar dangers from their own side, for a climate of *Feldjäger*-imposed terror also now engulfed them.

Maintenance

Like the other technical arms, the effectiveness of Germany's panzer troops owed much to their ability to keep vehicles and equipment in good working order, despite the burdens imposed by the battlefield. Every week, crews would spend many hours in the quiet periods between combat engagements working on maintaining their vehicle. Crews frequently had to undertake simple repairs on the engine, repaint flaking camouflage, or mend damaged track links. During the bitterly cold Soviet winters, tanks crews often had to start engines periodically during the night, or keep fires going under their vehicle to prevent both their engines and their anti-freeze from freezing solid.

Indeed, desperate mechanical improvisation in the field was the order of the day for most panzer units in all theatres of war. In the East during the spring of 1944, *SS-Oberscharführer* (Sergeant) Sepp Haffner, the engine mechanic of the 101st SS Heavy Tank Battalion, had to somehow repair a defective Tiger tank before an approaching Soviet T34 column reached the German position. Haffner quickly diagnosed a leaking cylinder head seal and hurriedly collected all available cigarette packets from the crews which he packed into the gaps in the cylinder head seal. This proved sufficient to restore the Tiger's mobility until it reached a nearby German field workshop. In addition, after 1942 recovery of disabled tanks became critical for the Germans as frontline losses decimated their available tank strengths. One Germany Army tank gunner corporal recalled that when the Tigers of the 3rd Company, 506th Heavy Tank Battalion moved across a steep railway embankment near Cisterna, Italy, on 23 May 1944 to engage Allied armour, two Tigers jammed their long, overhanging, 88mm gun barrels in the ground. Consequently, battalion workshop soldiers operating a Bergepanther recovery vehicle had to pull free the immobilised vehicles while under enemy fire before the approaching Allies reached them.

Logistics

Given the tempo of armoured operations, and the distances over which panzer divisions operated, Germans' ability to resupply them logistically proved the main constraint on their rate of advance. All panzer units possessed transport and supply units equipped with lorries and half-track tractors, but these were never available in large numbers. Whenever German armoured forces undertook strategic penetrations, their supply units had to improvise to keep the spearhead formations supplied with fuel, lubricants, ammunition and rations. As Otto Weber of the 10th Panzer Division recalled during Operation 'Barbarossa', the inability of the German logistic system to supply the rapidly advancing armoured forces led them to live off the land. Like all German formations in the East, the troops of the armoured divisions ruthlessly plundered the villages through which they advanced, seizing meat, bread, wheat, livestock and milk. The 18th Panzer Division, for example, requisitioned 40 tons of meat from the local population during November 1941 alone. To keep up their dwindling mobility, as winter arrived, armoured divisions increasingly requisitioned from local populations all the sledges, snow shoes, and felt boots that could be found. The panzer troops crushed any resistance they encountered. At Jarotin, near Kharkov, for example, soldiers burned down many straw and mud cottages.

During lulls in the fighting, commanders billeted their panzer troops in the mud and straw huts of Soviet peasants, the troops usually forcing out the occupants into the freezing Russian winter, where many thousands died of hunger and disease. In spring 1942, for example, Henry Metelmann's tank company took over as billets primitive Soviet mud cottages in the village of Rosenthal near Perekop in the eastern Crimea. Each tank crew, following their orders, occupied one mud hut and threw out the occupants. Metelmann's crew found 'their' cottage occupied by a Soviet women and three children: they simply gave the Russians five minutes to collect their possessions and leave, and did not even bother to watch the four heavily laden figures trudge out across the snow-laden landscape toward a very bleak future. Metelmann confessed to feeling somewhat uneasy about the fate of the occupants they had turfed out, but then the warm fire and the hot rations being prepared soon robbed his thoughts of any nagging doubts. This was war, after all, and such things happen, he rationalised, an attitude symptomatic of the harshness of the war on the Eastern Front.

During combat operations in the East, ration supplies available at the front frequently fell below authorised levels. To compensate, German soldiers went to great lengths to secure additional sources of food. When the 101st SS Heavy Tank Battalion halted in a Soviet village in early February 1944, they came across a pig, which they swiftly killed. One of the SS troopers produced a blow-torch and proceeded to singe off the hide, but before the hungry soldiers could cook the pig, a Russian tank column opened fire. As the Tiger tanks pulled out of the village to engage the tanks, the last vehicle could be seen with the pig, rolled up in a tent, attached to the rear of its

Right: A Tiger tank of the 101st SS Heavy Tank Battalion during the unit's approach march to the Normandy front in 1944.

turret. The mere presence of Soviet armour was not going to deprive the starving troopers of their prize find!

Panzergrenadiers

All-arms cooperation within the panzer division proved the key to German effectiveness. One crucial component of these divisions were the *panzergrenadiers* (motorised infantry), which cooperated intimately with the armour. In 1939,

German *panzergrenadiers* – then grouped in a rifle brigade – operated mainly in trucks, although a few half-tracked armoured personnel carriers (APCs) were also available. At this time, as one German private remembered, the Army used these half-tracked APCs simply as troop transporters to deliver and drop off riflemen at the edge of the battlefield: from here the grenadiers would close to join combat, after which they would return to rejoin their vehicles.

However, during the 1940 German invasion of the West, APC-mounted *panzergrenadiers* often moved forward in their vehicles alongside the armour during tactical engagements. In these battles, as section-leader *Gefreiter* (Corporal) Ulrich Stahl of the 5th Panzer Division recalled, they often provided intimate support for their armour, either from within their half-tracks, or while dismounted from their vehicles. In particular, they often provided screening duties on the

Left: The exhausted face of a decorated German tank commander standing in his cupola late in the war. Note the two sets of headphones that he is wearing. Infantry ride on the tank to provide support as necessary, as tanks fighting in built-up areas without infantry support were very vulnerable to enemy soldiers – as the Germans found to their cost in the battles for Stalingrad. This view clearly shows the commander's cupola, with its vision ports, and the battered remains of a crude white winter camouflage. German panzer crews had their own all-black uniform, with death's head badges on their collars and berets (not being worn here). The dark colour of the uniform helped hide any oil patches, a common hazard for tank crews.

flanks of advancing armoured wedges, or else debussed from their vehicles to mop up enemy stragglers. In 1940, however, the *panzergrenadiers* suffered only modest casualties performing these roles, since the ill-prepared Allies found it difficult to cope with the shock action inflicted by the German *Blitzkrieg*.

By Operation 'Barbarossa', half-track mounted *panzergrenadiers* had assumed major frontline combat roles, usually covering the flanks of armoured penetrations to prevent enemy counter-strokes. However, the increasing Soviet resistance encountered highlighted how vulnerable they, in their open-topped and thinly-armoured APCs, had become to enemy fire. Private Wilhelm Drabich of the 10th Panzer Division recalled the severe casualties that decimated his APC-mounted section during combat across terrain which had turned into a muddy morass in late October 1941, during Operation 'Typhoon', the German drive on Moscow.

Between 1942 and 1944, as the strategic initiative passed to the Allies, *panzergrenadier* tactics evolved. Increasing casualties led to fewer flank protection missions, Sergeant Stahl recollected, while instead *panzergrenadiers* often preceded the armour to neutralise enemy infantry equipped with hollow-charge anti-tank weapons. During 1945, half-track APCs reverted to their original role of transporting troops to the edge of the battlefield. Now, Stahl recollected, the *panzergrenadiers* de-bussed to fight in static defences, while their APCs – now often equipped with cannon rather than just machine guns – provided fire support from the rear.

Whatever the theatre, the climate, or the precise tactical role, the various troops that filled the ranks of Germany's panzer divisions nevertheless constituted a battlefield spearhead upon which Germany relied heavily during its protracted military campaigns of World War II. All-arms cooperation provided the key to their success, and in addition to *panzergrenadiers*, the self-propelled artillery within panzer divisions provided sterling support for the armour. It is thus to the experience of German artillery troops that this study now turns.

Artillery

Artillery was, next to the infantry, the second largest combat arm of the German Army during World War II. Having said that, however, the German artillery branch never reached the scale, in terms of resources and importance, as artillery did in the wartime American, British, and Soviet armies. The reason for this lay in the perceived lessons that the German military drew from World War I. German examination of the Great War raised doubts about the ability of artillery to win modern wars as they concluded that such weapons had proven unable to break the stalemate of trench warfare on the Western Front. Therefore, between the wars the German military directed considerable resources into novel new instruments of war – armoured forces and air power – that it hoped would revolutionise warfare, rather than to artillery.

The 1919 Treaty of Versailles placed further obstacles in the way of German artillery research and design between the wars. The treaty limited the number of such weapons Germany could field and forbade the deployment of mobile heavy artillery pieces entirely. Yet despite these restrictions, and in no small part because of them, the Germans intensively researched and designed innovative new artillery weapons during the 1920s.

The result of this technical innovation was the development of ordnance that would remain the mainstay of the German artillery arm throughout World War II. This ordnance included a horse-drawn 105mm light field howitzer, a manoeuvrable, rugged and reliable workhorse that became the mainstay of German field

Left: The four tank kill rings are clearly visible on this 8.8cm anti-aircraft gun deployed on the Eastern Front near Voronezh.

artillery throughout the war. The Germans also produced a robust, 150mm heavy field howitzer and a long-range 100mm heavy gun, both of which served until the end of the war. The Germans also experimented with rocket artillery, ultimately developing accurate fin-stabilised rockets as a vehicle to deliver poison gas and other chemical weapons. Thankfully Hitler – remembering his own experience of being temporarily blinded by gas in 1918 – refrained from using these stockpiles. All in all, the German artillery went to war better prepared than its enemies.

Having said this, there was little that was truly revolutionary about German artillery at the start of World War II and, in fact, it suffered from a number of significant deficiencies. In particular, the German Army lacked heavy motorised artillery. The Versailles restrictions ensured that the artillery arm constantly struggled to meet expansion needs during the 1930s. It was thus slow to motorise, had too little heavy artillery, and the bulk of artillery remained horse-drawn. These deficiencies reflected the widespread scepticism within the higher ranks of the German Army that artillery could be decisive in future wars. Instead the light field howitzer standardised in the 1930s was geared toward the fast, mobile operations that the German Army envisaged. An appropriate emphasis on manoeuvre and speed, many gunners mistakenly believed, would obviate the need for a powerful, centralised artillery arm. Instead the German Army envisaged the forward employment of artillery at the battalion and regimental level to disrupt and to harry, rather than shatter, an enemy already outmanoeuvred and unbalanced by fast-paced, deep-penetration ground offence.

Training

Another strength was the quality of German training as gunners underwent rigorous and realistic instruction. After having completed their three months of basic training, recruits who volunteered for the artillery progressed to another three months of branch instruction. One of the key characteristics of German training was overlap: recruits were taught to perform a variety of roles. Thus, for example, all gunners in horse-drawn units, like Alfred Knappe of the 24th 'Leipzig' Artillery Regiment, learned to ride and to look after the regiment's horses, as well as how to operate their howitzers. Initial fire drills, Knappe recalled, were carried out with dummy shells and bags of sawdust to imitate powder, aiming at a fixed point for practice. Each crew member learned a specialised role: the direction finder, for instance, handled the sighting and ranging of the guns. After gun crews had become proficient, they progressed to battery training. Knappe trained with the battery troop which was responsible for range-finding and obtaining information that the forward observer required. He also learned to do the observer's job in case the latter became incapacitated. Only when the battery was adjudged competent was it allowed to take part in field exercises.

Knappe also vividly recalled the intensity of his pre-war artillery officer training at the War Academy: each day he spent six hours in the classroom and three in the field. He complained about the length of the instructional day and the fatigue it induced. Knappe estimated after the war that during peacetime he never worked less than 10 hours each day, and sometimes 12 hours or more. He even had to train on Saturday mornings, he complained in a letter to his parents. Only when Germany went to war did Knappe appreciate the true value of his training. He came to see that one of the strengths of his instruction was its commitment to inter-arms cooperation as the key to effective artillery support. Thus Knappe and his fellow gunner officer candidates actually undertook extensive infantry training to acclimatise them to infantry thinking and procedures. He learned to view combat from the infantry officer's perspective, and to appreciate the difficulties the infantry faced, in order to support them more effectively in combat. The result was the instilling of intimate inter-arms coordination which became one of the cornerstones of German military effectiveness in World War II.

Knappe got to put his training to good use in the September 1939 Polish campaign, and it was precisely in the manner in which he had trained that the Germans used artillery in Poland. Armour played a major role in the German victory as mechanised forces penetrated deep into the Polish rear to disrupt their communications and paralyse the enemy until infantry and artillery could arrive to annihilate them. This combination allowed the Germans to rapidly overrun Poland at light cost. Though the campaign was short, it demonstrated a number of flaws in pre-war artillery thinking. Despite the doctrinal emphasis on rapid manoeuvre warfare, the infantry frequently operated along more traditional lines. Post-campaign analysis concluded that the infantry remained too dependent on artillery fire to smash enemy defenders. When artillery fire support was lacking, the infantry proved reluctant to press the attack. This proved to be the

Below: The best German heavy artillery weapon of the war, the 17cm Kanone 18 in Mörserlafette, seen here just before firing.

case, an after-action report observed, when the four light field howitzers of *Leutnant* (Lieutenant) Anton Dreschler's 2nd Battery, 28th Artillery Regiment were the only artillery support available for an attack by the 28th Reconnaissance Battalion at Podsosnina Lukowska on 15 September. Though Dreschler fired off his entire allocation of shells, the attack failed as, Dreschler believed, the infantry were unwilling to close with a well-entrenched enemy.

The heavy street fighting the Germans encountered in Warsaw, the Polish capital, also exposed the army's lack of heavy artillery. Built-up urban areas reduced the effectiveness of artillery fire as buildings absorbed significant damage, and debris blocked roads and provided excellent cover for a determined enemy. The consensus of gunner opinion was that horse-drawn teams found it difficult to deploy through the debris-strewn Warsaw suburbs to acquire new positions to fire on the city centre. Moreover,

Above: The gunner of a German light field gun looks through his optical sights during artillery training before the war.

cities greatly increase the difficulties of fire observation and direction. An anonymous gunner from an independent army artillery battalion that supported the assault on Warsaw – anonymity was after all conducive to candid answers – bemoaned the difficulties of locating targets and the enormous turnover in forward observation officers who repeatedly fell victim to well-concealed Polish snipers.

Though examination of the Polish campaign identified deficiencies in the army's artillery capability, the much greater military weaknesses of Germany's opponents obscured such deficiencies throughout the early war years. Thus artillery continued to play a secondary role dur-

ing the May–June 1940 Western Campaign as German armoured spearheads, ably supported by tactical aviation, outpaced the Anglo-French armies. Only on occasions did German artillery play a major combat role, such as during the 13 May storming of the Meuse River at Sedan. Artillery occasionally found itself called up to the frontline when German forces encountered heavy Allied armour – the French Char B2 and the British Matilda in particular – against which the existing German anti-tank and tank guns were impotent. The Germans got a real fright at Arras on 21 May 1940 when the British 7th Royal Tank Regiment launched a major counter-attack with 74 Matilda tanks into the flank of Erwin Rommel's 7th Panzer Division and rapidly overran his anti-tank companies. The unperturbable Rommel deployed several light field howitzer batteries of the 78th Motorised Artillery Regiment as part of an all-arms defensive force commanded by Major von Paris to thwart the thrust.

The German howitzers fired high explosive over open sights, gunner Otto Greim recalled, but proved unable to penetrate the heavy armour of the Matilda. At Wailly, German gunners began to desert their batteries in panic and, abandoned by his troops, von Paris sought safety in a cottage in nearby Beauvais only to have the Headquarters Group of the 8th Battalion, Durham Light Infantry commandeer the dwelling for their headquarters. For 24 hours the major hid beneath a bed as British officers came and went.

Rommel assumed personal command of the wavering scratch force. He gave the remaining guns individual targets and, by his very presence, kept them firing. His calm demeanour steadied the defenders and by sheer weight of fire they finally forced the British armour back, allowing Major von Paris to escape and rejoin his division! Thus, contrary to pre-war German thinking, the Germans learned in France in 1940 that properly led and deployed field artillery could be an effective antidote to armour on the battlefield.

As the Western campaign progressed, the ineffectiveness of even the heaviest German ordnance to destroy fortified defences also became apparent. It was attacks on isolated French forces in the Maginot Line that first exposed this weakness. On 15 June 1940 the 215th Artillery Regiment bombarded the Fort de Four à Chaux in the Vosges Mountains with a 355mm Czech Howitzer and the last surviving 420mm Big Bertha gun from World War I. However, the thick concrete walls of the fort proved impervious to German fire and its garrison held out until the French capitulation. Similarly, the 183rd Artillery Regiment attempted to silence a French 75mm gun emplacement on the Upper Rhine

front by surrounding the bunker and firing an 88mm anti-aircraft gun over open sights at point blank range into the rear of the emplacement. The German gunners gave up after exhausting their ammunition with no discernible effect.

Maginot surrender

The French use of firing from embrasures that could close when under enemy fire in fact made many of the batteries of the Maginot Line virtually impregnable to conventional artillery fire. On 18 June the Germans assaulted the Fort de Fermont behind a hail of fire from 305mm guns and 210mm howitzers, but the French kept their embrasures closed and no discernible damage was done. As soon as the firing stopped German infantry rushed its outer defences. The French immediately opened the embrasures of the fort's four 75mm guns and blasted the German attack to pieces: the French lost a single man killed during the day-long engagement. Recognising the futility of taking even an isolated fort on the Maginot Line, the Germans settled down to invest and starve out the garrison. It did not fall until days after France's capitulation when a French officer under a white flag persuaded the garrison that France had indeed surrendered.

German troops learned new lessons about the capabilities and limitations of artillery in North Africa, when in February 1941 Hitler sent a small motorised force under the leadership of the daring armoured commander, Erwin Rommel, to shore up the disintegrating Italian position in Libya. Since fighting in North Africa had been absent from Hitler's plans for world domination, the German military was not even remotely prepared for combat in desert conditions. This was especially true for German gunners who discovered that many of the basic assumptions of continental gunnery simply did not apply in North Africa. As Alfred Troppe concluded in a report summing up the consensus of gunner opinion, desert sand significantly reduced the explosive impact of artillery fire, frequent desert sandstorms badly hindered observation and fire-control, and artillery kicked up such large clouds of sand on firing that they became vulnerable to enemy counter-battery fire. All in all, the desert curtailed the traditional role of artillery.

But it was on the Eastern Front after 22 June 1941 when Hitler launched Operation 'Barbarossa' that German artillery encountered profound challenges. The Eastern Front proved very different from anything that German gunners had previously experienced as the size and diverse topography of the Soviet Union ultimately swallowed up the German advance. The defensive experiences of the thinly stretched German

infantry ultimately transformed Wehrmacht artillery practices. Widely dispersed, the infantry experienced defensive difficulties as they faced repeated Soviet counter-attacks that often employed heavy tanks. Combat quickly showed that infantry lacked anti-tank capability and had no effective counter to Soviet heavy armour. Bruno Wiesemann recollected that infantry divisions thus often had to deploy forward their field artillery in a direct-fire role to support the infantry and halt armoured penetrations, even

though this brought heavy loss of guns through close range line-of-sight engagements.

The Eastern Front was therefore physically and psychologically very different from previous German experience. Extensive swampy, primeval forest limited observation and reduced artillery effectiveness, provided excellent cover and concealment, and thus allowed the Soviets to harry and bleed the Germans. A vigorous partisan movement soon flourished behind the front and, Wiesemann recalled, artillery columns faced

Left: German civilians celebrate as an artillery tractor pulls a 15cm sFH 18 howitzer through the streets of Danzig in September 1939. A variety of means were used by the Wehrmacht *to pull artillery pieces, such as the half-tracks seen here, purpose-built artillery tractors and, increasingly as the war progressed and fuel shortages became more common, horses. In the parts of Poland that had been German before the Treaty of Versailles in 1919, the German invaders were welcomed as liberators by many of the inhabitants. Danzig (now Gdansk) had been declared a free city and, along with the 'Polish Corridor' giving Poland access to the Baltic Sea, cut off East Prussia from the remainder of Germany.*

ambushes. Russian winters posed particular problems for gunners: the terrible cold froze guns, and deep snow and ice immobilised many pieces. Even the horses proved unable to survive. Artillery completely lost the vital mobility for both its survival and its effective employment.

Catastrophic losses

By April 1942 the Army of the East, the *Ostheer*, had lost one quarter of the artillery that had begun the campaign. Even more catastrophic were the loss of towing tractors and horsed limber teams, significantly curtailing mobility. Declining troop strengths, artillery shortages, and limited mobility compromised the German defensive principles of manoeuvre and depth. Instead, troops had to rely on coordinated artillery fire to buttress static, fortified defences.

As the German defence of winter 1941–42 increasingly abandoned linear defence and resorted to improvised fortified village 'hedgehogs', troops abandoned the zones between these positions to the enemy. Lacking the manpower to close these gaps, the Germans relied on artillery, firing on pre-set coordinates, to repulse Soviet infiltration. Gunners also learned the necessity of stringent fire control and saw that concentrated fire could disrupt Soviet incursions. The result was the emergence of meticulous, integrated defensive fire-plans. As *Hauptmann* (Captain) Hederecker, a battalion commander in the 35th Artillery Regiment, reported, his gunners learned that a barrage on Soviet units forming up for an attack could stampede even the most experienced Soviet units. Thus by 1943 coordinated artillery fire had become the backbone of the German defence on the Eastern Front.

During 'Barbarossa' the Germans were again confronted with the problem of reducing heavily fortified defences. The solution was to dust off the mothballed siege artillery of the Great War, add new purpose-built railroad guns, and concentrate available super-heavy artillery to smash through the strongest reinforced concrete structures. The Germans assembled these super-heavy guns in spring 1942 for their assault on Sevastopol in the Crimea. The guns arrayed against the port included the Gamma Mortar, the Karl and Thor mortars, and the rail gun Dora. The Gamma Mortar, an offspring of the famous Big Bertha gun of the Great War, fired a 927-kg (2043-lb) shell to 14km (8.7 miles) and required 235 artillerymen to operate. However Gamma paled in comparison to the 61.5cm Karl and Thor which fired an incredible 2200-kg (4850-lb) shell. The Dora rail gun dwarfed even these pieces: at 80cm in calibre, Dora was the largest artillery piece of World War II and required no less than 60 rail cars to transport it. Its barrel was 32.5m (106.6ft) in length and fired just three 7.8-m, 4800-kg (10,582-kg) shells an hour! The gun ran on a standard, double-track rail line, and servicing, firing and maintaining this monster required 4000 personnel, including 1500 gunners.

The Germans employed this super-heavy artillery to destroy the formidable Maxim Gorky

Below: Gunners prepare to fire their 21cm Kanone 38 heavy artillery weapon against the American bridgehead at Anzio in 1944.

Fort in Sevastopol. This fort, built in 1934 and cut two storeys deep into the base rock beneath the city, was one of the world's strongest. It contained two 305mm guns protected by up to 4m (13ft) of concrete and an additional 30cm (11.8in) of steel. Its guns had a range of 44km (27.3 miles) and, from November 1941, had proven to be the bane of the German assault on Sevastopol, constantly harassing and disrupting German attacks. But from May 1942 it found itself targeted by the German siege guns which knocked out first one, and then the other gun of the fort. Backed by intense bombardment, German assault engineers fought their way into the fort's underground corridors to take the strongpoint in bloody hand-to-hand combat. The fall of Maxim Gorky was a turning point in the siege and hastened the Soviet decision to evacuate the city.

Mortars and rockets

As Germany became locked in a bitter, attritional struggle that it ultimately could not win, a significant change in German artillery force structure emerged as it shifted toward greater use of mortars and rocket-launchers. These were cheaper and faster to build, mobile, easier to camouflage and conceal, yet delivered a comparable 'weight of shell' as conventional artillery. German troops increasingly relied on mortars, which they used to great effect for fire support in the latter stages of the war. German units had more and heavier calibre mortars than the Allies, and they were less vulnerable to air attack. By 1944 mortars had become the mainstay of German indirect fire support and, in Normandy, inflicted 70 per cent of Allied casualties. The German 81mm medium mortar was allocated to the heavy weapons companies of German infantry battalions and offered sterling service. In 1943 the Germans introduced the lethal 120mm heavy mortar that replaced 150mm heavy infantry guns in select regimental cannon companies.

From 1942 the German Army also increasingly used the Nebelwerfer multi-barrelled rocket-launcher for indirect fire support. It soon proved one of the most effective weapons in the German arsenal as it could quickly bring down consider-

Above: Mountain troops man their light moun-
tain gun in Italy during the summer of 1944.
Such terrain was a common feature in Italy.

able firepower. Enemy troops everywhere came to dread Nebelwerfer 'stonks' – with the demoralising 'wail' of the projectiles in flight – which often stopped enemy assaults and frequently routed the enemy. Yet the weapon's short-range, ravenous munitions consumption, and tell-tale dust cloud on firing, which made it vulnerable to detection, were significant tactical limitations.

Typical of the impact of rocket artillery was the use of the 52nd Rocket Launcher Regiment in action in the bitter fighting for the Russian city of Voronezh on the Don River during summer 1942. Facing bitter resistance, the infantry demanded greater fire support and received a regiment of heavy 210mm rocket-launchers. Kurt Gieseler recalled that the regiment arrived during the

evening before the planned attack and deployed on a flat, open plain. At 0130 hours three rocket batteries unleashed a one-hour barrage to soften the defenders. According to one of the grenadiers waiting to attack, the sight was awe-inspiring and the sound nerve shattering. He described the noise as a low-pitched howling that quickly rose to a screaming crescendo as huge bursts of flame shot from the launchers as they fired their rockets in succession. The blast from a full salvo from all five barrels was so powerful that it would overturn the launcher. A staggered salvo's blast was still so great that the crews had to take cover in trenches before firing to avoid incineration.

Lines of flame with trailing clouds of red smoke marked their route as the rockets streaked across the sky, Gieseler later recalled. The ground shook for miles around under their impact. The same grenadier recorded in fascinated awe the impact of the barrage: it turned the

Above: Artillery troops from the SS Totenkopf *Division bombard Soviet positions with their 15cm sFH 18 howitzer.*

ground into a moonscape and fires burned fiercely in many places. The salvoes so demoralised and concussed the enemy that the Soviet troops were unable to resist. The instant fuses used and the resultant blast created a terrible concussive effect, the grenadier recollected, and the heavy barrage caused such variations of air pressure that it literally sucked air out of men's lungs and suffocated them to death. Others were so concussed that they were driven insane and ran uncaring toward German lines where they were shot down. The regiment's awesome firepower helped break the back of Soviet resistance and contributed to the final capture of Voronezh.

Despite increased use of mortars and rockets, the impact of German artillery on the battlefield dwindled in the latter stages of the war. Allied aerial mastery and German shortages increasingly rendered German artillery ineffective and it was less able to buttress defences successfully. Allied airpower hampered German artillery to an unprecedented degree as air attacks repeatedly

suppressed artillery fire, and forced guns to redeploy often and to adopt elaborate camouflage and concealment. The air threat, combined with munitions shortages, meant that the Germans had to abandon massed fire and resort to 'shoot-and-scoot' tactics, and random 'sprinkling fire' with individual guns. At the same time, ammunition shortages denied the Germans the concentrated barrages needed to repulse Allied attacks. Massed fire became rare and artillery units increasingly abandoned counter-battery fire altogether as a waste of munitions. Moreover, poor ground observation, lack of air observation or photo-reconnaissance, and inadequate signals communications all hampered German artillery operations. On the relatively few occasions where the Germans were able to mass artillery support and resupply it, such fire support buttressed their defence. But the Germans were able to do this successfully less and less often.

Defensive success

One example of German defensive artillery success came in the opening stages of the 1944 Normandy campaign in the Cotentin Peninsula. American troops had rapidly established themselves ashore on D-Day at 'Utah' beach and quickly consolidated their beachhead. Thereafter they moved inland towards Cherbourg, their objective. However, in mid-June the Germans temporarily checked the American advance along the Quineville Ridge and in front of the communications hub of Montebourg. The Germans realised that holding this last defensive position before Cherbourg was crucial if they were to deny the port to the Allies. They thus reinforced their defences by concentrating a 19-gun artillery group commanded by Major Friedrich Kuppers.

As American forces assaulted the Quineville Ridge between 10 and 14 June, the greatly outnumbered German defenders found their flanks hanging in the air. In this crisis, gunner Gerhard Bauer recalled, Kuppers received permission to fire without restraint, a rare order that reflected the seriousness of the German situation. Kuppers' 19 guns blasted away, raining such a deluge of well-aimed fire down on the American spearheads that their attack wavered. The American advance guard pulled back and assumed defensive positions. Kuppers' guns had made a signal contribution in halting, albeit temporarily, the American advance. Concentrated artillery fire had bought the German defenders precious time, time to bring up new reinforcements from the 77th Infantry Division and reinforce the thin defensive crust that blocked the approaches to the great prize: Cherbourg.

Artillery Group Kuppers had already used daring tactics to thwart the American attempt to overrun the isolated St Marcouf naval artillery battery which was proving a thorn in the side of all American attempts to press northward. Irritated, the Americans determined to eliminate the threat at whatever cost. *Marine Leutnant* (Lieutenant) Ohmsen, the battery commander,

found his men pinned in their underground bunkers as American troops overran the battery and began to eliminate the emplacements by thrusting detonation charges through the apertures and firing slits of the battery bunkers. In a desperate effort to evade incineration, Ohmsen called down the fire of Kuppers' guns on his own positions. The ground trembled as the accurately placed fire pounded the battery position, sweeping away the Americans on top of the bunkers as the assault broke up and the survivors fled.

Skilful and judicious use of defensive artillery fire, the Germans learned, could bring defensive successes out of all proportion to the resources expended. Another favourite German artillery tactic was to place defensive artillery fire behind an Allied rolling barrage to hit the following infantry. Such tactics suggested to Allied infantry that their friendly fire had fallen short, greatly increasing the demoralisation effect. Whereas infantry frequently ploughed on through enemy fire, they invariably went to ground or retreated if they thought that their own artillery was hitting them. Thus a few well-timed shells could stall an entire attack.

This was the case during the Canadian attack on Carpiquet airfield west of Caen on 4 July 1944. The Germans had held this position since D-Day, preventing all Anglo-Canadian efforts to outflank Caen from the west. On 3 July the small defending garrison from the fanatical 12th SS Panzer Division *Hitlerjugend* realised another Canadian attack was imminent. *SS-Rottenführer* (Corporal) Fritz Eckstein remembered how every available German gun fired at the most likely enemy forming-up points and so badly disrupted one Canadian battalion that it could not advance. When another battalion moved toward the village behind a rolling barrage, the Germans laid fire behind the barrage. Believing themselves to be under friendly fire, the enraged unit retired in disorder. Once more well-placed fire saved the day and bought a little more precious time. But time would ultimately run out. Increasingly out of ammunition and lacking transportation, the German artillery arm disintegrated in the final bitter battles of spring 1945.

Airborne and Special Forces

Germany deployed a variety of airborne and special forces in World War II, including navy 'K-men' armed with human torpedoes for use against Allied vessels at anchor, the airforce's KG-200 unit, Werewolf 'stay-behind' commandos, and SS special forces. This chapter concentrates on German paratroops and Brandenburg commandos.

Paratroop origins

In the 1920s, the Soviet Union experimented with soldiers dropped from aircraft by parachute. In these trials, the 'paratroopers' held on to the wings of the aeroplanes and slid off at the required height. Soon, more effective tactics evolved and suitable aeroplanes took the paratroopers up in 'sticks' inside the aeroplanes prior to jumping. German officers attached to the Red Army in the 1920s viewed these trials with interest and in the 1930s, with German rearmament under Hitler, the German airforce (*Luftwaffe*) developed an airborne force commanded by Major-General Kurt Student. Volunteers for this force completed a vigorous training programme followed by six jumps before becoming a *Fallschirmjäger*, a member of Germany's elite paratroop force. The failure rate for potential

Left: Trainee German paratroops line up to board their transport aircraft during a practice jump in an early part of the war.

Right: Trainee para-troops make their first practice jumps from specially-designed platforms within large Air Force hangars. The troops were taught how to exit safely from an aircraft, and how to position themselves during their descent. Landing techniques were also taught, but injuries were still commonplace due to the high speed of descent of the German parachutes.

paratroopers was high, and deaths and serious injury from training accidents remained common. The realistic training and elite status of the German paratroopers made them some of the toughest and most effective soldiers of the war.

German paratroopers usually jumped from Junkers Ju-52 transport aircraft that carried 17 fully laden paratroops to a distance of 1370km (850 miles). The paratroops landed with only what they carried: small arms, grenades, and machine guns. To overcome this lack of firepower, Student used a specially designed glider, the DFS 230, to carry additional troops and heavier equipment. When towed by an unladen Ju-52, the DFS 230 lifted troops or freight up to 1135kg (2500lb). As will be seen with the battle for Crete in 1941, the lack of organic firepower would be one of the paratroopers' biggest handicaps.

In September 1939, when war broke out, the Germans had available the 7th Airborne Division for air assault operations. In addition, there existed the 22nd Air-Landing Division, under army rather than airforce control, but still available for combined airborne operations. While the German Army had drawn up plans to use paratroopers operationally against Austria and Czechoslovakia between 1938 and 1939, it first used airborne forces in September 1939 against

Poland. While the air drops in the Polish campaign were minor compared to later campaigns, they still contributed to the breaking of Polish morale. One military historian later observed that in order to promote sabotage and treachery behind the Polish front, the Germans made a number of air landings and parachutist drops near Polish army headquarters which disrupted their chain of command and threw the mobilisation process into confusion.

Following their limited deployment in Poland, the Germans then used their airborne units in the invasion of Denmark and Norway in April 1940 where paratroopers secured Sole airfield near Stavanger ahead of the main invasion force. The airborne landings in Norway played a vital part in securing airfields for air-landing reinforcements. This was the first real strategic deployment of airborne forces with paratroopers projected far from home.

Victory in the West

When it came to invading the Low Countries and France in May 1940, the Germans used all their available paratroopers for maximum effect. For the attack, the Germans deployed airborne and special forces in three roles: firstly, special forces for behind-the-lines interdiction and for securing key transport junctions; secondly, airborne forces to capture Belgian border fortresses; thirdly, airborne units to secure bridges and airfields in Holland ahead of the main German land invasion. In total, the Germans had available 4500 trained parachutists formed into five battalions. The remaining airborne troops, some 12,000 men, were carried in gliders or aircraft.

In May 1940, the Germans employed 4000 of these paratroopers against three key Dutch airfields ringing the Hague (Ockenburg, Ypenburg and Valkenburg), and to secure nearby bridges across the River Maas at Rotterdam, Dordrecht and Moerdijk. The remaining 500 dropped on and around the Belgian border fortress of Eben Emael. Student's attacking force for the Dutch airfields and bridges comprised four parachute battalions and one air-transported infantry regi-

Below: German paratroops, this time landed by glider, practise rapid deployment after landing during training.

ment of three battalions. Though they suffered heavy losses, the force achieved its objectives. Student, himself wounded in the head by a Dutch sniper during the attack, remembered that his forces dared not fail, for if they did, the whole invasion would have failed. Meanwhile, the Germans used the remaining parachute battalion in a daring *coup de main* operation against the Hague to capture the Dutch government. Although foiled, this attack caused much confusion and showed the willingness of the Germans to push their airborne forces to the limit.

Eben Emael

The Germans used the remaining 500 paratroopers of Student's force in an even more audacious attack to capture the Belgian fort of Eben Emael and two nearby bridges over the Albert Canal that were vital for the German offensive's success. The fort blocked the German invasion routes into Belgium and the French High Command believed that Eben Emael could hold

the Germans for five days. Yet it was neutralised in the space of a few hours by a daring German airborne assault and fell a day later. Completed in 1935, Eben Emael guarded crossings of the Albert Canal and the approaches to the city of Liège. Protected by an enormous cutting that fell 36.5m (120ft) in a sheer drop to the Albert Canal, the fort measured some 823m x 640m (900yds x 700yds). In a series of single and double turrets in the fort, the Belgians had mounted artillery pieces from 75mm to 120mm. There were, in

addition to the main armament, numerous light cannon, machine guns, and a supporting battalion of infantry secure in underground bunkers. While Eben Emael seemed an invincible stronghold, it had an Achilles' heel: it possessed no anti-aircraft defences. It was this omission that gave the Germans the idea of using their airborne forces to take the fort.

Since November 1939, a party of German combat engineer volunteers trained in utmost secrecy under the overall command of *Hauptmann*

(Captain) Koch for a special airborne drop. Allowed no leave and forbidden to mix with other units, the members of Storm Detachment Koch were sworn to secrecy under pain of death. They practised attacking mock-up and captured Czech Sudeten forts until, on 10 May 1940, 78 of them took off from Cologne in 11 gliders towed by Ju-52s. By using gliders with expert pilots, the Germans could cover the 21km (13 miles) from the German–Belgian border to Eben Emael in silence and remain unseen, so landing on top of

Left: German para-troopers involved in the attack on Eben Emael pose with a war correspondent. The Germans hurried-ly removed the gliders used in the attack on the Belgian fort to encourage speculation about how this supposedly impreg-nable fortress was taken so rapidly. The attack also saw the first use of hollow charge explosives in war, allowing the German paratroops to destroy the Belgian gun emplacements with relatively light equipment. Overall the German airborne forces were a great success in 1940, significantly speeding the German advance into the Low Countries. Germany was quick to use them for propaganda pur-poses, and the threat of more landings dam-aged enemy morale.

the fort. With superb timing, Koch's force crash-landed on Eben Emael just five minutes before the bulk of the *Wehrmacht* crossed the border. The fort's Belgian sentries saw nothing until the gliders landed on its roof.

The expedition commander, *Leutnant* (Lieutenant) Rudolf Witzig, was lost when his glider tow-rope snapped over Cologne. However, Witzig and his men, with commendable energy, prepared a landing field by chopping down willow hedges, and called in another Ju-52. By the time Witzig arrived over Eben Emael, however, the remainder of the force, under the able command of Witzig's sergeant-major, *Oberfeldwebel* Wenzel, had already begun overwhelming the Belgian defenders using (for the first time) powerful hol-low-charge explosives to blast through the thick, steel carapace of the fort. The twin-120mm tur-rets proved too much even for hollow-charge explosives and so were despatched by simply pushing explosives down the gun barrels.

Meanwhile, other gliders landed close by at the bridges over the Albert Canal and, with the garrison of Eben Emael under attack, were able to secure these strategic crossing points. Through the night of 10/11 May, the Germans on and in Eben Emael held on until advancing infantry of the German Sixth Army helped force the fort's surrender the next day. For the cost of six dead, Koch's airborne unit had spearheaded the cap-ture of a supposedly impregnable fort and helped capture over 1000 Belgian troops. Hitler's delight at the fall of Eben Emael was immense: it was a bold coup that breached the Albert Canal defences. Hitler rewarded two soldiers of the Storm Detachment Koch with Knight's Crosses, Germany's highest military decorations.

Other airborne special operations

While Eben Emael remains the most famous German use of airborne troops, the *Wehrmacht* employed other airborne assaults in the spring of 1940. For instance, as the first German troops crossed into Luxembourg, there were already *Wehrmacht* soldiers behind enemy lines. Some had gone in previously as tourists, while others had been brought in by plane. Led by *Leutnant*

(Lieutenant) Hedderich, 125 volunteers landed in 25 Fiesler Storch light planes on the Franco–Luxembourg border near Esch-sur-Alzette with the aim of securing a vital junction. After turning back a number of Luxembourg workers cycling to collect their weekend pay packets, Hedderich's group was ordered to leave by a local police officer. Hedderich's men arrested the confused policeman, secured communications, and then awaited the main body of German troops advancing by road.

Specially trained troops of the elite *Grossdeutschland* infantry regiment conducted a similar operation farther north in Belgium.

Below: A German paratrooper, with his parachute harness strapped across his chest, prepares to jump out of a Junkers Ju 52 transport plane.

Known as Operation 'Niwi', Fiesler Storch planes landed 400 soldiers to secure communications in front of the main armoured advance. The Germans landed in the Belgium Ardennes near the villages of Nives and Witry (hence the code-name 'Niwi') to protect the road links through the Ardennes for the vitally important German push on Sedan. While the landing at Witry went according to schedule, the force for Nives was beset with problems that showed how easily an airborne operation could go awry. A sergeant with the force recalled that, soon after take-off, his and two other aircraft lost sight of the other Storchs, then eventually landed in the wrong place, only to take off again. The lost planes landed to meet once again with stunned locals who told them that they were again at the wrong place. The Germans eventually found their target and captured Witry after a short fire-fight with Chasseurs Ardennais. They were later relieved by German armour.

Impact of airborne troops

It is noteworthy that on the whole front of the German invasion, the defenders blew every bridge according to plan, except where airborne forces were used. The effect of the landings was not just material but also psychological. The Germans were careful to suppress the information about how hollow-charge explosives helped capture Eben Emael. Thus, the Allies feared that their enemy had used some special weapon such as nerve gas. With their reliance on the Maginot Line, the French were particularly worried by the fall of Eben Emael. If the Germans could deal so quickly with the world's strongest fort, what would be the fate of the Maginot Line?

All-in-all, the use of airborne forces in Belgium and Holland spread a panic among the Allied troops that aided the German attack. The ability of gliders and paratroopers to land behind enemy lines, along with the use of German Brandenburg commandos disguised as Dutch troops (see below), led to a paranoia about 'Fifth Columnists' such as nuns in hobnailed boots or priests with hidden machine-pistols. In front of the advancing Wehrmacht there spread a wave of panic that demoralised and paralysed as much as any Stuka dive-bomber or advancing panzer. The limited use of airborne troops was in extraordinary contrast to the exaggerated reports at the time of German parachutists. Part of the explanation for the panic caused by the threat of airborne forces can be found in the widespread use by the Germans of dummy paratroopers dropped behind enemy lines (a trick copied by the Allies in Normandy in 1944). This ruse proved most effective, helped by the natural tendency of heated imaginations to multiply figures.

This fear of airborne forces spread to Britain once France had fallen and the British Army had been evacuated from the beaches of Dunkirk. British troops dug ditches across open land and left cars as obstacles in fields to prevent glider troops landing. The fear of paratroops was not unfounded: had the German invasion of Britain – codenamed Operation 'Sealion' – gone ahead, the plan was for the 7th Airborne Division to land ahead of the main landing force in Kent behind the towns of Hythe and Folkestone to prepare the way for the invasion force coming by sea. The defeat of the *Luftwaffe* in the summer of 1940, and Hitler's interest in attacking the Soviet Union, led to the cancellation of the invasion. The German paratroops detailed for the attack on Britain were now given their boldest task: Operation 'Mercury', the invasion of Crete.

Crete, 1941

If one battle symbolised the German paratroopers' war, it was the battle for Crete. Fought by the paratroops of the 7th Airborne Division, supported after the initial landings by the 5th and 6th Mountain Divisions (one attached regiment), the invasion of Crete followed the successful German occupation of Greece (where paratroopers captured the Corinth Canal). The proposal was for Student's paratroops to land by parachute and glider on the three main airfields of Crete at Maleme, Heraklion and Retimo, and to then be supported by light mountain troops (*Gebirgsjäger*) arriving by sea and transport aircraft once the airfields were secured. The mountain troops were used as the 22nd Air-Landing Division was

Above: After Crete the airborne forces were used as ground troops. Here paratroops take advantage of a break in the shelling to repair trenches.

delayed in Bulgaria and so was unavailable. This was a daring proposal and potentially fatal for the German paratroops. They would have to overcome opposition from the 35,000-strong British and Commonwealth garrison on Crete who actually knew, through Ultra intelligence, of the impending invasion.

The paratroops suffered horrendous casualties from the more heavily armed defenders who poured fire into the slow-moving Ju-52s from which the paras jumped. The heaviest fighting was at Maleme airfield where an elite paratroop assault regiment went in at dawn on 20 May 1941. German fighters and dive-bombers provided what support they could but without heavy weapons the paratroops were fighting at a disadvantage. The airborne force arrived in a mix of gliders and parachutes to be met with a curtain

of fire. As the paratroops descended, many wildly fired their Schmeissers, but as one account put it, 'many found graves where they found earth'. Koch, the hero of Eben Emael, landed with the 3rd Company, and worked to destroy the anti-aircraft positions around Maleme.

Those airborne forces fared best that landed away from British and Commonwealth troop concentrations and were able to get to their weapons canisters. The high fighting spirit of the para-troopers along with disparate enemy resistance eventually allowed the Germans to build an 'air head' for the mountain troops arriving in Ju-52s which crash-landed on the fireswept airfields (some mountain troops tried to come by sea in improvised invasion fleets but were intercepted by the Royal Navy). Eventually the Germans forced the Allies back to the southern port of Sphakia where the majority of the force was evacuated by sea. But the cost of the German vic-

Left: The immaculately presented Colonel Brauer, cigarette holder in one hand, gives orders to his men during the battle for Crete. The struggle for Crete cost the German airborne forces dearly in terms of casualties, and as a consequence Hitler determined never to use large-scale paratroop landings in future campaigns. Had the Allied commanders been more aggressive in their counter-attacks, the paratroopers could have been eliminated and the invasion a failure. The paratroopers' reputation as hard fighters stood them in good stead when defending the monastery of Monte Cassino in 1944. They managed to delay significantly the Allied advance northwards through Italy, though they again suffered high losses.

the Führer at his Rastenburg headquarters. Hitler told Student that 'Crete has shown that the day of the paratroops is over. Paratroops are a weapon of surprise, and the surprise factor has been overplayed.' Student expanded on this conversation after the war when he remembered how 'over the next few months when the call came for paratroops to fight on the ground, I was to realise the significance of his words.'

As ground troops, the paratroops fought with distinction in all the major theatres of war: the Russian steppe, the rocky djebel of Tunisia, the hills of Italy, and the bocage of Normandy. But Crete was the last divisional-sized drop of the *Fallschirmjäger*. In 1943 the 7th Parachute Division was renamed the 1st Parachute Division and a further nine parachute divisions were raised for use as ground troops. As the First Parachute Army, these units fought with distinction in Italy and northwest Europe. Paratroops were, however, still occasionally employed in smaller units for airborne operations, most famously in the Ardennes during the 'Battle of the Bulge' in mid-December 1944.

The Battle of the Bulge

In December 1944, the Germans launched their last major offensive of the war in the West with a thrust aimed at Antwerp. After some initial success, the Americans first contained and then pushed back the Germans who suffered heavy and irreplaceable losses. As part of the Ardennes offensive, or 'Battle of the Bulge', the Germans deployed both paratroopers and special forces. The special forces – *SS-Standartenführer* (Colonel) Otto Skorzeny's 150th Panzer Brigade – had the task of infiltrating behind enemy lines to confuse and harry American units. More significantly, there was also a battalion-sized paratroop drop during the offensive. Known as Operation 'Stösser', and led by the Crete paratroop veteran *Oberst* (Colonel) Baron von der Heydte, the aim was to land a force to seize the Malmédy road junction ahead of *Generaloberst* (Colonel-General) Sepp Dietrich's Sixth Panzer Army. There were echoes here of the successful drops of 1940. But this time the Allies had the initiative

tory was tremendous. By the end, the 7th Airborne Division had ceased to exist as a fighting formation. In total, German casualties exceeded 7000, with over 4000 dead and missing. The bulk of these casualties came from the paratroop and glider-force that had landed in the first few days.

Crete was thus the paratroopers' swan-song. On 19 July 1941, when Operation 'Barbarossa' was a month old, paratroopers awarded the Knight's Cross for valour at Crete paraded before

and the paratroop battalion was a newly formed unit dropping over heavily wooded terrain.

D-Day for the operation was 16 December 1944. It was then delayed because of a lack of fuel needed to take the force to the airfield. High winds then confused the pilots who dropped von der Heydte's paratroops in the wrong place: many landed in Germany, some in Holland. In the end, von der Heydte gathered 125 paratroopers who had landed near to Malmédy. Von der Heydte was himself in great pain from an arm shattered in a training exercise, his men were without any heavy weapons, and the radios for communication with Sixth Panzer Army were broken. As a consequence, the paratroopers were unable to take the road junction. It was all very different from the heady days of 1940 and 1941.

Meanwhile, the Americans believed that a whole paratroop division had landed and rushed troops to the area. The *Luftwaffe* failed to air-drop supplies to the beleaguered paratroops and so, on 21 December, von der Heydte ordered his men to attempt to break out in small parties through the American lines. However, von der Heydte and most of his men were captured. Germany's last airborne operation achieved little except to sow some ephemeral panic behind enemy lines. The operation showed that, for a successful drop, good planning, surprise and an overall strategy were vital. With Germany retreating on all fronts in late 1944, the drop at the Battle of the Bulge was doomed to failure.

Brandenburg Commandos

The Brandenburg special forces originated in a unit with the cover name of *Bau- und Lehrkompanie Brandenburg* which was established at the time of the 1938 Czech crisis by Captain Theodor von Hippel. This officer had fought in Lettow-Vorbeck's guerrilla campaign in German East Africa during World War I against the British. In 1938 he came up with the idea of sending troops behind Czech lines to join up with German Sudetens. With the Munich settlement this idea was put on hold but the German intelligence service, the *Abwehr*, headed by Admiral Wilhelm Canaris, looked to use the Brandenburg

battalion in the invasion of Denmark, Norway, the Low Countries and France in 1940.

The Brandenburgers' mission was to secure strategic objectives before the main push, by posing in enemy uniforms and speaking their language to achieve surprise. In April 1940 the Brandenburgers went into action for the first time by seizing the Danish Belt bridge. Subsequent actions met with mixed results. The attempt to seize the bridges over the Maas River was a disaster: there was a shoot-out in which the leader of the bogus Dutch soldiers, Brandenburg *Leutnant* (Lieutenant) Hocke, was shot. It was impossible to remove the explosives placed by the Dutch and three key bridges were destroyed in front of the advancing panzers. The time it took to throw an assault bridge across the Maas led to long tailbacks of tanks and delays to the German advance. It was obvious that successful Brandenburg behind-the-lines operations could make or break an operation. Again, at Arnhem in Holland, there was a fiasco where Brandenburgers made up for the lack of fake Dutch uniforms by making outlandish cardboard versions of Dutch helmets. The fake disguises were easily spotted and the Brandenburgers driven off.

At Gennep in Holland the Brandenburgers were more successful. Under the command of *Leutnant* (Lieutenant) Walther, three Brandenburgers posed as Dutch police officers escorting a group of German prisoners of war. These POWs had hidden small arms and succeeded in securing the bridge from the surprised defenders. This showed what the Brandenburgers could achieve, for across the bridge went the armour of the 9th Panzer Division that separated the Dutch Army from the French Seventh Army pushing east. Brandenburgers were also responsible for securing some 24 objectives in Belgium ahead of the panzers. Here the Brandenburgers were largely successful and 3rd Company, Brandenburg battalion, received no fewer than 92 Iron Crosses for their actions in these few vital days.

After France's fall the Brandenburgers expanded beyond battalion strength and fought in the Balkan campaign, securing the Ploesti oil-fields of Romania and the River Vardar crossing in Yugoslavia. By late 1941 the Brandenburgers had attached other specialist units such as a marine battalion and a parachute battalion. Brandenburgers were employed for a variety of special missions (such as the capture of Lwów in 1941) on the Eastern Front, and in North Africa. Brandenburg paratroops were also involved in recapturing the islands of Kos and Leros in 1943 where they suffered heavy casualties.

By the end of 1942 the Brandenburgers were regrouped as *Sonderverband* (Special Formation) 800 with a complement of five regiments. This then evolved into the Brandenburg Division. The division, however, was controlled from Berlin and deployed in widely scattered packets over all theatres of war. The controversial methods employed by the Brandenburgers, along with the precious use of scarce matèriel that Brandenburg operations involved, often made them unpopular with other Germans, especially as the spectacular suc-

Below: Brandenburg commandos, dressed in Red Army uniforms and using a Soviet truck, prepare to undertake a covert operation in autumn 1941.

cesses of the early years of the war were offset by later failures. After the 20 July 1944 bomb plot against Hitler, the SS took over the *Abwehr* and the unit was reorganised as a *panzergrenadier* division. It fought on the Eastern Front until the end of the war. Only the *Kurfürst* Regiment retained a commando role. Some of the experienced Brandenburg commandos however chose to join the SS raiding formations (*Jagdverbände*).

The English Patient

As has been seen, Brandenburgers fought in all theatres of war. In North Africa they tried to cut the Allied supply route that ran from Nigeria to Egypt across the Sahara desert. In addition, the Brandenburgers took two *Abwehr* agents to Egypt, accompanied by *Hauptmann* (Captain) Count Almasy, the man immortalised in the film *The English Patient*. The count helped direct the Brandenburgers and the two agents to Assuit in Egypt. While the agents successfully took the train into Cairo, they were later picked up by the British. Almasy and the Brandenburgers returned to German lines.

The Waffen-SS

The SS (*Schutzstaffel*) constituted the spearhead political movement of the German Nazi Party, and those individuals who voluntarily joined it supported passionately the Nazis' racist ideology. After Hitler's rise to power in 1933, the Nazis sought forcibly to rearrange the European Balance of Power to create a 'New Order' which would be cleansed of Jewish influence and dominated by a 1000-year Third Reich. The military wing of the SS, the *Waffen-SS* (armed SS), was created in March 1940 by amalgamating the existing SS paramilitary organisations: the Führer's bodyguard (SS *Leibstandarte Adolf Hitler*); the SS Special Readiness (*Verfügungs*) Division; and the Death's Head (*Totenkopf*) concentration camp guards. During the 1939–45 war, the armed SS was dominated by two key characteristics: first, many *Waffen-SS* formations delivered impressive combat performances because their soldiers displayed great determination, bravery, tactical skill and camaraderie; second, the *Waffen-SS* constituted a fanatical, highly politicised, force determined to achieve the Nazi regime's brutal ambitions and to crush mercilessly its enemies.

During World War II the *Waffen-SS* changed into a force with little in common with the embryonic organisation of 1939. The million-strong *Waffen-SS* of 1945 comprised a heterogeneous collection of varying races and formations. The

Left: Troops of the SS Liebstandarte Adolf Hitler *parade at Berlin Templehof airport in 1935 to mark the arrival of the British foreign minister,*

half-dozen 'classic' Aryan *Waffen-SS* forces – such as the SS *Leibstandarte, Das Reich, Totenkopf*, and *Wiking* Divisions – usually performed impressively on the battlefield. In the East between 1941 and 1942, amid appalling conditions, these divisions established the military reputation of the *Waffen-SS*, and consequently Hitler ordered further expansion and mechanisation of the organisation.

From 1942, Himmler's ambitions to increase his SS empire led to the creation of many new, less well-equipped, 'divisions' raised from the ethnic Germans of central Europe, from 'racially acceptable' volunteers (like Walloons and Balts), and from 'racially inferior' Slavs (such as Albanians, Russians, and Uzbeks). Though these units often performed poorly in combat, they gave sterling service in the racial war of annihilation

Below: Soldiers of the Liebstandarte *parade in front of their barracks at Lichterfelde in Berlin during 1939.*

the Nazis unleashed in the Axis-occupied Soviet Union. Soldiers of formations like the SS *Florian Geyer* Division massacred captured partisans and cooperated with the genocidal *Einsatzgruppen* murder squads. Four of these Special Task Groups, which included *Waffen-SS* troops, executed by shooting some 1.5 million Jews and Communists in the East between 1941 and 1943. Right through until 1945, Himmler continued to create a motley collection of new SS 'divisions', increasingly raised from inferior sources such as trainees, stragglers and former convicts. The very worst of these units, the 'Kaminski' and 'Dirlewanger' Brigades, were fit only for savage anti-partisan sweeps, during which they behaved with such appalling brutality that even mainstream *Waffen-SS* fanatics wished rid of them! Clearly, the heterogeneous 1945 *Waffen-SS* bore scant resemblance to the racially pure Aryan elite force of 1939.

While significant elements of the *Waffen-SS* did constitute a battlefield military elite, the organisation as a whole was a dual politico-military institution committed to lead the Nazis' bloody internal and external struggles. Membership of the armed SS brought the prospect of service, albeit temporary, in the wider SS. Convalescing *Waffen-SS* troopers, for example, participated in the Nazi Holocaust against the Jews through service as guards at the heinous extermination camps like Auschwitz.

Training and indoctrination

Many *Waffen-SS* soldiers, like 20 year-old *SS-Schütze* (Private) Erich Holzer of the 'Totenkopf', fervently believed the racist, expansionist, anti-Semitic and anti-Communist ideas that dominated the Nazi world view. Until 1942, acceptance into the *Waffen-SS* as a recruit or an officer cadet was far from easy: height restrictions applied, and favourable interviews and references were required, as was a lengthy proven Aryan ancestry. Initially, for example, the *Leibstandarte* only took soldiers who were at least 1.87m (6ft 2in) tall. From 1942, these requirements were increasingly relaxed as Himmler tapped new sources of recruits from ethnic German and non-

Aryan sources to avoid direct competition with the *Wehrmacht* over scarce manpower resources.

Often imbued with profound arrogance, many *Waffen-SS* soldiers, like radio operator *SS-Panzerschütze* Friedrich Werner of the *Leibstandarte*, perceived themselves as the vanguard warriors of a racially superior Aryan German *Volk* (people) locked in a desperate fight for survival. Their historic mission was to spearhead the Nazis' creation by conquest of a new Nazi European Order; if Germany's enemies resisted, the *Waffen-SS* soldier would crush them without mercy. To carry out their mission, SS troops had to possess utter determination and a lack of mercy. Tank loader *SS-Sturmann* (Lance Corporal) Ewald Graf recalled that the brutal training regime through which all *Waffen-SS* troops passed certainly helped instil these qualities. SS training, pioneered before 1939 by officers such as Felix Steiner at the Officer Cadet Schools at Bad Tölz and Brunswick, based itself on the principles of iron discipline, imbuing an elite *esprit de corps*, and political indoctrination.

This training was also based on realistic, live-fire, combat simulation, so realistic, in fact, that SS commanders accepted a 10 per cent casualty rate during training as a matter of routine. Tank loader *SS-Rottenführer* (Senior Corporal) Paul Rohlweder vividly recalled that he, like many *Waffen-SS* recruits, had become well acquainted with the horrors of the battlefield long before he reached the front. This iron determination was often reflected in the way in which commanders drove on their soldiers. One SS *Leibstandarte* trooper recalled that during the April 1940 German invasion of Greece, *SS-Sturmbannführer* (Major) Kurt Meyer drove on his troops' advance by dropping a primed grenade behind the last men.

Protracted section and unit training, such as that which the 2nd SS Panzer Division *Das Reich* undertook during winter 1943–44, sought to create both strong small unit (sectional) cohesion and a larger-scale *esprit de corps*. For the *Das Reich* Division, recalled artillery commander *SS-Standartenführer* (Colonel) Karl Kreutz, this was particularly necessary since many of its latest

*Above: SS Officer Cadets attend a lecture at the Officer Training School (*Junkerschule*) at Bad Tölz, near Munich.*

recruits were forcibly conscripted ethnic Germans from eastern Europe, hardly the best potential soldiers. As will be seen, the success of the *Das Reich* in bonding these modestly motivated recruits into their respective sections was demonstrated by the role these troops played during the reprisal actions the *Das Reich* undertook against French civilians on its mid-June 1944 march to the Normandy front.

SS political indoctrination, *Leibstandarte* tank driver *SS-Sturmann* (Lance Corporal) Franz Ellmer clearly remembered, was instilled less through formal instruction, but rather by placing a heavy onus on instructors and commanding officers to seize every moment to stimulate ideological discussion in an informal atmosphere. Official guidelines instructed commanders to use personal conversations with subordinates and

informal leisure hour discussions as a vehicle for political indoctrination. In general, officer-man relations were more intimate in the *Waffen-SS* than was normal within the rest of the German armed forces. The chaplain *Kapitän* Karl Ossenkop observed during 1944 that a particularly informal and close relationship existed in the 5th SS Panzer Division *Wiking* between the officers and their ethnically mixed Scandinavian, Dutch and Walloon soldiers. Moreover, as one SS trooper in the 10th SS Panzer Division *Frundsberg* recalled, between 1943 and 1944, historical instruction was based around a few simplistic historical anecdotes that served to instil pride in the German *Volk*, and the belief that the Führer would lead the nation to victory. Above all, this trooper recalled, these discussions was intended to instil in the men a profound hatred for all of Germany's enemies: not just the Slavs, but the British and Americans as well. This animosity manifested itself repeatedly on the battlefield when SS soldiers inflicted atrocities against enemy prisoners or civilians.

Above: An SS Hauptsturmführer *interrogates a Red Army prisoner on the Eastern Front in the summer of 1944.*

Other aspects of the *Waffen-SS* training regimen, however, undermined rather than bolstered the poor combat performance of the 'racially inferior' formations like the Albanian *Skanderbeg* Mountain Division. The virulent racism and abuse meted out to non-Aryan recruits during training by the Aryan *Waffen-SS* instructors did little to establish good cohesion within these far from promising formations. Consequently, some formations experienced significant problems with low morale and high desertion rates. Some troops of the SS East Turkish Volunteer Formation even mutinied. Furthermore, even supposedly 'racially equal' SS volunteer units like the Finnish Volunteer Battalion and the Scandinavian *Wiking* Division, experienced problems with the retention of volunteers after their recruits had tasted the full venom of bigoted German SS instructors. *SS-Sturmbannführer* (Major) Georg

Eberhardt witnessed first-hand that many *Wiking* recruits refused to extend their original service agreements after repeated verbal abuse and extra punishment details coming from their bigoted SS instructors.

Soldiers of destruction

The creation of a highly politicised and brutally trained military force which was institutionalised around obedience to orders, fanaticism and ruthlessness, led to the combat experience of the *Waffen-SS* being stained with numerous atrocities. In every single theatre that *Waffen-SS* units served, their soldiers carried out war crimes against partisans, enemy prisoners of war, and civilians, in violation of both international law and the existing norms of war. As early as the September 1939 Polish campaign, the SS *Verfügungs* Division, the *Leibstandarte*, and the *Totenkopf* concentration camp guard units followed the frontline units and led the Nazi campaign to murder thousands of Jews, Polish intellectuals, businessmen and other 'leadership cadres'. In one incident, troops of the *Leibstandarte* herded 50 Polish Jews into a synagogue and killed them. In France during May 1940, soldiers of the SS *Totenkopf* Division, led by Fritz Knöchlein, murdered 100 British prisoners of the 2 Royal Norfolks at Le Paradis Farm, while in a similar incident at Wormhoudt, *Leibstandarte* soldiers forced 80 prisoners of the 2nd Warwicks into a barn and killed them with grenades and small-arms fire.

During Operation 'Barbarossa', the June 1941 Axis onslaught against the Soviet Union, frontline *Waffen-SS* units executed Bolshevik party political commissars serving with Red Army units, and frequently executed Soviet prisoners. Moreover, armed SS personnel served with the four genocidal *Einsatzgruppen*, which operated behind the advancing German forces to execute 1.5 million Soviet Jews and other 'racial undesirables' between 1941 and 1943.

Waffen-SS atrocities occurred less frequently in the West than in the Soviet Union, but several appalling acts of brutality against innocent civilians still took place. Perhaps the worst such incident was committed by troops of the 2nd SS Panzer Division *Das Reich*. The formation reached the Normandy front in late June 1944, after a protracted approach march from the south of France. During this redeployment its troops committed several appalling atrocities against innocent French civilians in reprisal for Resistance attacks that killed several SS soldiers. The worst excess occurred on 10 June 1944 at Oradour-sûr-Glane, where SS soldiers led by *SS-Sturmbannführer* (Major) Otto Dickmann, shot or burnt to death 642 unarmed civilians in four hours of ruthless savagery. Some 15 of the key participants in the massacre, including *SS-Unterscharführer* (Sergeant) Boos, were the Division's Alsatian troops who had been conscripted against their will in 1943. By 1944, these recent Alsatian conscripts were fully assimilated into its sectional primary groups, and were keen to prove their loyalty to their section comrades by being even more robust against Germany's enemies than their ideologically motivated peers.

Fine combat performances

This political indoctrination also led to fanatical individual combat performances from many *Waffen-SS* troops, like that of *SS-Schütze* (Private) Emil Dürr of the 12th SS Panzer Division *Hitlerjugend*. During the late June 1944 British 'Epsom' offensive west of Caen, Dürr lay in wait for an approaching column of Sherman tanks at the side of a sunken Bocage lane. With his Panzerfaust, Dürr disabled the second Sherman, and then raced out to finish off the stricken vehicle by placing a 'sticky bomb' against the vehicle's side. The device fell off, however, and so the SS trooper snatched it up and held it against the side of the tank until the bomb exploded, destroying the Sherman but killing Dürr in the process. Such self-sacrifice might help slow the Allied advance in Normandy, but could not alter the battlefield reality that overwhelming Allied numerical superiority would eventually bring them decisive success.

Perhaps the most famous display of outstanding *Waffen-SS* combat performance was the bloody repulse inflicted on the 7th Armoured

Division – the famous 'Desert Rats' – by Michael Wittmann's Tigers at Villers Bocage on 13 July 1944. At this time *SS-Obersturmführer* (Lieutenant) Michael Wittmann commanded the 2nd Company, 101st SS Heavy Tank Battalion, with 14 Tigers on strength. By his death on 8 August 1944, Wittmann had become Germany's leading tank ace, and had received the coveted Knight's Cross with Swords and Oak Leaves for his 139 'kills' against enemy armour. On 13 June 1944, Wittman's command Tiger spotted through the summer haze a squadron of the British 22nd Armoured Brigade moving east beyond Villers Bocage deep into the German rear. Wittman's gunner, *SS-Oberscharführer* (Senior Sergeant) Balthasar Woll, himself an accomplished Eastern Front veteran, cursed the apparent complacency that characterised the British advance. Wittmann and his accompanying four Tigers moved off down the hill into Villers Bocage to cut behind the British squadron. In the town, Woll's excellent gunnery swiftly destroyed three of four Churchill tanks that engaged the German tank. Next the Tiger headed east back up the hill to deal with the lead squadron, which remained unaware of the German presence in the area. Wittmann approached the British squadron from behind and advanced along the armoured column so that Woll could pour round after round into the stricken vehicles. Within two minutes Wittmann's tank had destroyed 13 British vehicles. His four other Tigers soon joined the action, and by the time the Tigers withdrew, 28 burning British vehicles littered the battlefield.

Wittman, two other Tigers and a newly arrived Panzer IV next headed back to Villers Bocage. In the meantime, a 76.2mm(17pdr) Sherman Firefly tank plus three Churchills, together with a 57mm (6pdr) anti-tank gun had assumed ambush positions in side-streets on the premise that Wittmann would return. As Wittmann's command Tiger rumbled down the street, the British anti-tank gun engaged the tank and disabled it,

Right: Behind the front line in the Soviet Union, German security troops frequently summarily executed any 'suspects' they encountered.

forcing the tank ace, Balthasar Woll, and the rest of the crew to flee on foot to the safety of the German lines. Overall, for the loss of four of the 13 Tigers involved, Wittman's Tigers mauled the majority of a British brigade, destroying 40 vehicles in the process.

Tough missions

Given the elite status, ideological motivation and harsh training of the *Waffen-SS*, the High Command often allocated its soldiers the toughest military missions. The troops of the SS *Totenkopf* Division, in particular, experienced a particularly gruelling nightmare over the bitter winter of 1941–42. In December 1941, the Soviet counter-offensive in front of Moscow pushed back the Germans positions on either flank of Demyansk until the town was connected to the main German front by a thin 19.3-km (12-mile) deep salient. Throughout much of 1942, the Soviets repeatedly flung themselves against the precarious defensive positions held by the *Totenkopf*. During this protracted nightmarish experience, *SS-Sturmbannführer* (Major) Karl Ullrich recalled, the division suffered appallingly high casualties, and its emaciated, frost-bitten, lice-infested, disease-ridden SS troopers continued to suffer because the German High Command refused the formation permission to recuperate behind the frontline.

Conditions for other SS troops on the Eastern Front were often equally appalling. *SS-Obersturmführer* (Lieutenant) Hans Werner Woltersdorf of the SS *Das Reich* Division recalled that, during 1942, virtually all his platoon comrades were infested with lice. Every few months, during brief rest periods out of the line, the bedraggled and filthy SS troopers received new clothes. The men soon learned, however, that the lice much preferred their new, clean underwear to filthy old ones. In an attempt to reduce the problem, Woltersdorf recollected, his colleagues tied fresh bandages around their necks a few days

Left: The 1944 Warsaw Uprising was put down by some of the most unsavoury units linked with the Waffen-SS, *such as the* Kaminski *brigade.*

before receiving any new clothing. Large numbers of their lice migrated to the fresh bandages, which could be removed and burned to reduce the lice population before new clothes were donned. The unsanitary conditions in which SS soldiers often had to fight in the East also brought very real dangers of contagious epidemics. In Easter 1944, while resting at Odessa, Woltersdorf succumbed to cholera, and spent two weeks in a state of delirium with a raging temperature before medication fought off the disease.

Armoured spearhead

Increasingly from 1943, Hitler came to entrust the classic *Waffen-SS* armoured divisions with the spearhead role in German offensives, like those at Kharkov (spring 1943), Kursk (July 1943), and in Hungary (March 1945). In early 1943, the 1st, 2nd and 3rd SS *Panzergrenadier* (Mechanised) Divisions returned to the Eastern Front as part of the newly constituted SS Panzer Corps. They spearheaded Field-Marshal Erich von Manstein's highly successful counter-stroke at Kharkov that smashed the over-extended Soviet offensive across the Ukraine. This impressive achievement further enhanced the military reputation of the armed SS, but unfortunately it went hand-in-hand with a series of appalling crimes that the fanatical SS soldiers perpetrated against Soviet civilians or prisoners.

Subsequently, Hitler selected the SS Panzer Corps to spearhead the abortive German July 1943 Kursk offensive. Yet fine individual SS performances, like that of *SS-Unterscharführer* (Sergeant) Franz Staudegger of the *Leibstandarte*, could not rescue the ill-conceived offensive from abject failure. Similarly, in December 1944, the SS-dominated Sixth Panzer Army led the ill-fated German Ardennes counter-attack in the west, before Hitler transferred the formation east to lead Germany's last major offensive of the war, the 'Spring Awakening' operation in Hungary during March 1945. Indeed, when the faithful *Waffen-SS* failed to stem the Soviet push into Austria, an incensed Hitler ordered his elite SS divisions to surrender their distinctive armbands as a punishment for their failure. The use

Above: Close-up view of a Panzer IV of the 9th SS Panzer Division Hohenstaufen *at Lisieux, France, in June 1944.*

of these SS formations as 'fire brigades' rushed from one crisis to another only served to exacerbate the high exhaustion and casualty rates among their soldiers.

Special operations

Apart from its spearhead frontline role, the dual politico-military nature of the *Waffen-SS* meant that Hitler often tasked its soldiers with special operations of a more political nature designed to protect the Reich's internal security. Several units, such as the *SS Jagdverband Mitte* (Raiding Formation Centre), were configured as rapid reaction commandos for internal policing operations. One such occasion occurred on 20 September 1944, when the Führer ordered *SS-Standartenführer* (Colonel) Otto Skorzeny, his commando operations specialist, to devise contingency plans to keep Germany's wavering Hungarian Axis ally in the war against the

Soviets. These fears were realised when, in mid-October 1944, the Hungarian regime announced an imminent armistice with the Soviets, and ordered their troops to defend Budapest against a possible German intervention.

Skorzeny's SS forces then carried out a stunning coup, codenamed Operation 'Panzerfaust', to seize the Burgberg fortress in Budapest, the seat of the Hungarian regime. Skorzeny's troops included elements of the elite 600th SS Paratroop Battalion and SS Raiding Formation Centre, together with 35 *Wehrmacht* King Tiger tanks. One of Skorzeny's troopers recalled clearly the strong psychological impact exerted on the Hungarians by the physical presence of the supporting King Tiger tanks, as the SS commandos audaciously stormed the Burgberg. Within 30 minutes, the trooper recollected, his comrades had secured control of the seat of the Hungarian Government. The Germans then established Ference Szalasi and his Fascist Arrow Cross Party cabinet as the new regime in Hungary, so that they would continue the struggle against the advancing Red Army.

Retribution

Not surprisingly, the vicious war waged by the *Waffen-SS* between 1939 and 1945 inevitably led their personnel to be treated more harshly than *Wehrmacht* soldiers if they fell into enemy hands. This was particularly true of the Red Army and the various partisans operating in the Balkans, who both regularly executed or mistreated SS prisoners. Given these risks, it became a crucial element of the tactical ethos of the *Waffen-SS* to recover wounded soldiers from the battlefield despite the dangers involved. *SS-Obersturmführer* (Lieutenant) Woltersdorf of the *Das Reich* remembered one such incident on the Eastern Front in the Bulitschety Forest, near Zhitomir, on Christmas Day 1943. A Soviet attack left Woltersdorf – together with Wachter, his compa-

ny commander, and four soldiers – trapped behind enemy lines. As the group tried to escape, they were spotted by a group of Soviet soldiers in the distance, who opened fire. Wachter was hit in the ankle and could move only at a slow, and agonising, hobble. Instead of abandoning him, the other five risked their own lives by engaging in a fire-fight with a numerically superior group of Russian infantry, while two men helped Wachter deeper into the forest and safety. Repeatedly the injured officer urged his comrades to leave him behind, but they steadfastly refused to let him be captured. One of the group, sent ahead, managed

Below: Troops of the 2nd SS Panzer Division Das Reich *grab some rest next to a typical Norman stone wall in France.*

to intercept a German staff car, which sped down a nearby track to rescue the remaining five, including Wachter, from the pursuing Soviet troops. The next day, in a forward field hospital, German medics amputated Wachter's foot.

Fear of Soviet mistreatment led many SS troops on the Eastern Front to commit suicide rather than allow themselves to fall into enemy hands. By 12 February 1945, for example, the resistance of the SS-dominated German garrison encircled in Budapest had crumbled. Rather than allow himself to be taken alive by the Red Army, the wounded *SS-Oberführer* (Brigadier) Joachim Rumohr, commander of the 8th SS Cavalry Division *Florian Geyer*, committed suicide with his pistol, an example followed by dozens of his troops. *SS-Rottenführer* (Senior Corporal) Franz Josef Dreike of the *Das Reich* recalled that it became common practice for SS troops to make a pact that if one of them was badly wounded and could not be rescued, his comrades would finish him off with a bullet rather than allow him to be captured by the Soviets.

Such concerns loomed even larger during the first days of May 1945, as the Nazi Reich teetered on the brink of defeat. In the last hours of the war before Germany's 8 May 1945 surrender, large numbers of SS officers and men changed into Wehrmacht uniforms to avoid the likely retribution. Their chief problem was the conspicuous blood-group type all *Waffen-SS* personnel had tattooed on the underside of their upper left arm. Some SS soldiers burned off or cut out the mark, but this left a scar as evidence of their attempt to disguise their true identities. In early May 1945, as *SS-Obersturmführer* (Lieutenant) Woltersdorf recuperated after losing his leg in combat, he heard of more bizarre methods of disguising the tattoo. Woltersdorf ended the war at a *Wehrmacht* convalescent hospital at Beneschau in Czechoslovakia, and here he met SS colleagues who steamed their tattoos with smoking nitric acid to fade the mark, and others who repeatedly

Left: Michael Wittmann, an SS panzer ace, sits astride the 8.8cm gun of his Tiger I tank in a photograph posed for propaganda purposes.

applied corn plasters to remove the top layers of skin one by one, thus leaving less of a scar. The blood-group tattoo proved the bane of SS personnel trying to disguise themselves as *Wehrmacht* soldiers. At an American POW camp, Woltersdorf heard about a 'German Army' officer with no legs and only one arm who was sent to the SS internment camp at Mauthausen. Unfortunately, his only surviving limb just happened to be the one with the scar of his burned-off SS blood group.

In the last days of the war, the 3rd SS Panzer Division *Totenkopf*, like many of its sister formations, fled west to surrender to the Americans rather than the Soviets. Instead of being held in an American POW camp, the officers and men were delivered back to the Soviets. In retribution for the numerous war crimes the troops of the *Totenkopf* committed in the East, the Soviets sentenced many of the division's soldiers to long periods in labour camps, and executed many senior officers, including *SS-Brigadeführer* (Major-General) Hellmuth Becker. A similarly unpleasant retribution awaited troops of the 7th SS Volunteer Mountain Division *Prinz Eugen* who surrendered to Yugoslav National Liberation Army forces at Cilli, in Slovenia, at the end of the war. This division had earned itself a reputation for appalling brutality during the bloody anti-partisan war the Germans waged in the Balkans: mass reprisal hangings and burning down entire villages were their trademark. Once the Germans had surrendered, however, the partisans exacted retribution by executing dozens of their prisoners after drumhead trials.

The troops of the *Waffen-SS* had varied experiences during World War II, whether it be stubborn defence amid the frozen Soviet wastes, mass murder with the *Einsatzgruppen* behind the lines in the East, summary executions of partisans in the Balkans, or spearheading resistance to the Allied advance in Normandy. The common thread among the varied experiences of the *Waffen-SS*, the fanatical spearhead troops of the Third Reich, is suffering: the battlefield suffering the troops experienced themselves, but above all, the brutal suffering they so ruthlessly inflicted on Nazi Germany's enemies.

Casualties of War

A mong the most valuable and respected members of the German Army were the 'Sanis', the medical personnel whose devotion the troops eulogised in the affectionate satirical song about *Sanitätsgefreiter* (Medical Corporal) Neumann who purportedly had a magical healing salve that could fix any injury. Medical personnel were distinguished by their dark blue arm-of-service shoulder patches and by the Red Cross armband that they wore. According to international law, medical personnel were classified as non-combatants and they were therefore not supposed to be armed. However, particularly in the vicious war on the Eastern Front where neither side upheld established laws of war, German medical personnel frequently carried side-arms.

This was the case of Medical Sergeant Walter Hoffmann, who tended American paratroopers captured behind strong-point W5 on the south-eastern fringe of the Cotentin Peninsula in Normandy on the morning of 6 June 1944. Hoffmann, a veteran of the Eastern Front, had developed the habit of packing a Walther P008 Luger pistol, the favourite – if not the best – side-arm in the German arsenal. The senior American paratroop captain complained to the strong-point commander, *Leutnant* (Second Lieutenant) Arthur Jahnke, about this violation of international law, and the lieutenant made the reluctant doctor remove his pistol. Grumbling, Hoffmann remarked that he hoped the enemy would recognise him as a non-combatant. His hopes were

Left: German prisoners who volunteered to work in an American field hospital during the summer of 1944 queue up for a meal in the mess

soon dashed, however, for hours later Hoffmann was killed during the bombardment that preceded the landing at 'Utah' beach.

Medics undertook the herculean wartime task of treating both military and civilian casualties. The scale of this effort was enormous: armed forces medical staff treated almost 53 million casualties during the war. Despite the enormous strain placed on available resources, the quality of German medical care – even in the most primitive conditions – remained high. A wounded soldier who reached a field hospital had a 98.5 per cent chance of survival, testimony to the professionalism of German doctors and nurses.

Combat injuries

Any soldier injured was supposed to promptly remove himself – or be removed if he was unable to do so himself – to the unit's first aid post where

Below: Medical orderlies inject a wounded SS grenadier lying on a stretcher during the Normandy campaign of 1944.

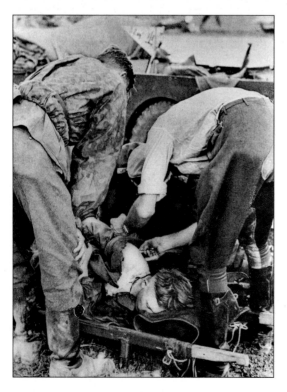

medics would evaluate his injuries and administer appropriate treatment. Those deemed only lightly wounded were immediately treated and then returned to their formations. Whenever possible, units endeavoured to hold on to their wounded personnel because once a soldier left his unit to receive medical treatment, there was always the risk that he might be posted elsewhere. Thus units preferred to treat patients 'in house'. These practices are illuminated by the experiences of a pair of SS grenadiers, Kurt Breitmoser and Leo Freund, who became impromptu anti-tank gunners manning a 7.5cm Pak 40 heavy anti-tank gun at the Chateau du Fosse, near St Sylvain, Normandy, on 8 August 1944. When the crew of the anti-tank gun they were protecting was killed by shrapnel, Breitmoser and Freund manned the undamaged gun. With beginners' luck, the two novice gunners destroyed a Polish Sherman tank with their first shot. After one more shot, however, their position was hit; Breitmoser was knocked unconscious and Freund wounded. Freund immediately dragged himself off to the nearest first aid post, where his light shrapnel wounds were cleaned and bandaged. His injuries were deemed sufficiently light not to dispatch him to the rear and by the time Freund returned with two stretcher-bearers to assist his fallen comrade, Breitmoser had regained consciousness, and together the pair re-manned the gun.

For more serious injuries, soldiers were evacuated to regimental or divisional aid stations. The seriously wounded were usually removed to an army hospital in the rear. Convalescents requiring longer periods of more specialised rehabilitation were generally transferred to hospitals in their home military district. Some 86 per cent of wounded returned to duty within three months and 99 per cent within six months. Less than one per cent were so badly maimed that they had to be discharged as unfit for duty. Many others returned to restricted duty in the rear or in an administrative post. On average, a wounded soldier spent nine days in hospital.

Once sufficiently recovered to be discharged from hospital, convalescents were usually posted

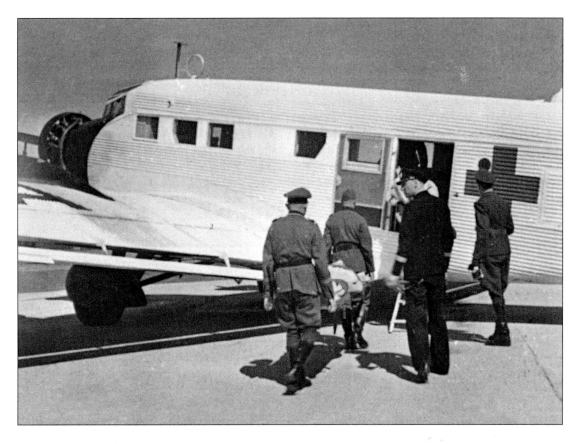

Above: Medical staff carry a stretcher case to the waiting Junkers Ju 52 air ambulance, clearly marked in Red Cross colours.

to convalescent units, where they undertook light military duties while they completed their recovery. If they had returned to Germany for hospitalisation, they transferred on discharge to the depot battalion affiliated to their unit and joined a convalescent company. These soldiers helped instruct new recruits in the battalion's training companies. Once recovered, convalescents often returned to the front mixed in with fresh recruits in so-called 'Marsch' (march) battalions.

On the other hand, the less seriously wounded who remained in the theatre of operations often temporarily joined field convalescent companies in the rear of the front where they would take on light guard duties until they were fully fit. Since there was always a danger of being assigned to a different formation from a field convalescent company, wounded soldiers often endeavoured to return to their original unit at their earliest opportunity, even when they were not fully recovered, and little was done to halt this practice.

The functioning of these medical evacuation procedures is well illustrated by the experience of *Oberleutnant* (Lieutenant) Siegfried Knappe of the 24th Artillery Regiment. On 14 June 1940 during the German invasion of the West, Knappe was hit in the wrist by a machine-gun bullet at Tremblay on the Ourcq Canal. Medical corpsmen bandaged the wound and administered morphine in the field. They deemed the injury serious enough to order Knappe's immediate evacuation. An ambulance transferred Knappe to a regimental aid station a few miles behind the front. Here a doctor evaluated Knappe's injuries and administered a tetanus injection and antibiotics to prevent infection. Knappe was then taken to an army field hospital at Noyen where he was sedated for the night. The next morning he was flown to a hospital in Bonn where doctors re-evaluated his condition. After the swelling had receded some three weeks later, Knappe had a cast fitted and was transferred to a hospital at Leipzig, his home town and also close to his regimental depot. After the cast was removed, Knappe underwent physical therapy to recover the mobility lost as a result of shattered bones and damaged nerves. It was not until September 1940 that army doctors considered him sufficiently recovered to return to his unit in conquered France.

One soldier who refused to leave his unit 'family' even to receive proper medical care was a young Flemish volunteer, Private Remi Schrijnen. On 3 March 1944, Schrijnen was wounded for the seventh time and, as previously, refused all entreaties by medical staff to go to a field hospital for adequate treatment. Instead, Schrijnen insisted on being patched up at a forward aid post and remaining with his unit. He was assigned to light duty and forbidden to approach the front while he convalesced. But when, three days later, his entire gun crew was killed, Remi set out for the front and single-handedly manned his still-intact gun. He waged an apparently hopeless battle against an entire battalion of Soviet armour. Schrijnen single-handedly destroyed 11 enemy tanks before being seriously wounded. A relief force found him unconscious and close to death the next day when a counter-attack reoccupied the battery position. This time Schrijnen had no choice but to accept evacuation to a rear hospital where he was patched up for the eighth time and underwent a long convalescence. During this convalescence, Hitler personally presented Schrijnen with the Knight's Cross, one of only a handful of privates ever to receive this highest award for gallantry.

Hospital ships

Like all combatants, the Germans utilised a variety of maritime vessels as hospital ships. The prominent display of Red Cross symbols was not always sufficient to protect a ship from attack. Indeed, the Soviet Government refused to recognise any German hospital ships, citing – with some justification – Germany's manifest violation of existing international laws. The British Government also refused to recognise small German hospital ships under a certain tonnage and attacked them. Though this was in violation of the Hague Convention, the British Government's position was that the primary purpose of such small hospitals ships was in effect to

Left: A wounded soldier is carried on a stretcher to a nearby field dressing station by his comrades. Other injured German soldiers capable of walking follow behind. The quality of treatment for wounded German soldiers on the battlefield was, overall, very high. This was important for maintaining good morale amongst the troops in the Wehrmacht.

Above: German soldiers fraternise with a group of surprisingly cheerful-looking Dutch prisoners of war during the May 1940 campaign.

rescue downed German pilots, the role of a glorified sea rescue launch, which was not entitled to protection under existing international law.

One such hospital ship that fell into this category was the small steamer *Rostock* which plied between France's Western Atlantic ports and Germany. *Oberst* (Colonel) Kaumann, the fortress commander of encircled Lorient who was wounded in late August 1944, was evacuated in early September 1944 on the *Rostock*. Despite its clear Red Cross symbols, British torpedo boats intercepted the vessel off Lorient and threatened to sink it unless the ship interned itself in a British port. With no escape, its captain complied and the torpedo boats escorted the ship to a British port where Colonel Kaumann and over 300 POWs were interned. Thereafter, the vessel was allowed to proceed to Germany. This 'illegal' detainment

precipitated a violent protest by the German Government which it lodged with the protecting power, neutral Switzerland, in Geneva.

Psychiatric illness

One area where the German medical profession remained backward was in its recognition and treatment of mental and non-combat injuries. 'Battle fatigue' was not officially recognised in the German Army. Men displaying nervous symptoms were classified as either mentally or nervously ill. The first category was much rarer; only about one in 500 soldiers who served in the war were classified as mentally ill. Nervous complaints were much more common, one man in 20 being so diagnosed during the war. The nervously ill were further subdivided into those with hysteria and those suffering from shock.

Informally, many troop commanders did their utmost to help and protect troops suffering from battle fatigue by issuing them special leave, reassigning them from the front to other duties in the rear for rest and recuperation. Within a soldier's own squad – his military family – squad leaders helped those under strain by re-assigning them to the least dangerous tasks, such as bringing up ammunition. Apart from these measures, there was not a whole lot a commander could do with men clearly on the verge of a breakdown. The Germans, however, retained a very macho – and rather unscientific – attitude toward battle fatigue. Many a soldier executed for cowardice had simply reached the end of his tether.

The lesson learned from World War I was not to send battle fatigue sufferers home for treatment, because their presence had a disconcerting and negative effect on civilians. Psychological casualties really only began to emerge for the first time in significant numbers during the Eastern Campaign. Some nervously ill patients required psychiatric treatment which included

Below: A young Soviet soldier with a PPSh 41 sub-machine gun guards a large group of bedraggled Wehrmacht *prisoners of war.*

electric shock therapy and hypnosis. Such treatments were surprisingly successful: some 85 per cent of cases returned to combat duty from one hospital for which records survive.

Desertion

Sometimes the psychological strain of combat proved too much for certain individuals and the result could be desertion. Having said this, in general the German military experienced very low rates of desertion. The military culture and the prestige associated with soldiering exerted enormous pressures against desertion which was treated as a heinous crime. Both the military and the state went to great lengths to apprehend and to severely punish deserters. Consequently, a soldier considering desertion had to contend with potentially hostile reactions from family, friends and acquaintances, any of whom might denounce him. Indeed, one of the greatest obstacles against desertion was the reality that the deserter had little prospect of evading the authorities in the long run. At the end of 1944, for example, there

were only five German Army officer deserters who remained unaccounted for.

Illustrative of the potential pitfalls and hazards of attempted desertion was the fate of *SS-Gruppenführer* (General) Hermann Fegelein, a high-ranking Nazi officer who had married Eva Braun's sister, placing him in Hitler's personal entourage. When Hitler decided on 20 April 1945 to stay in Berlin and die, Fegelein, his adjutant, had other ideas. Recognising the war was lost, he hatched a rather ill-conceived plan to lay low until Berlin had fallen to the Soviets. Hitler, with his pedantic obsession with detail, immediately noticed Fegelein's absence and sent out SS guards to find him. He was found in civilian clothes with a passport and foreign currency in his possession: incriminating evidence of intended flight. Fegelein was summarily condemned to death and immediately executed by firing squad.

The easiest way to 'desert' was always on the battlefield by surrendering to the enemy. Of course, such a strategy entailed considerable risk for a deserter, who faced being shot by either side. Indeed, German troops often fired upon their own soldiers attempting to surrender, and were encouraged to do so. The fate of the elderly reservists of a fortress battalion at Fort Westeck during the defence of the port of Cherbourg, Normandy, in late June 1944 illustrates such risks. As American troops attempted to storm the fort on 24 June, the embattled crew of a 75mm gun on the west of the fort endured more punishment than the elderly reservists could bear. They had been hit by air strikes and heavy artillery that chipped large chunks of concrete from the ceiling of their bunker, causing numerous superficial injuries, temporary deafness and concussion among the elderly crew, many of which had not fought since the Great War. But it was the approach of American engineers with flamethrowers and assault charges that panicked the gunners. Fearful of being incinerated, the crew tied a white sheet to a rifle and hung it out the gun embrasure. In the fort's underground command bunker, a lieutenant on periscope duty laconically reported to the fort commander: 'White flag on gun embrasure West.' The com-

Above: A black British soldier is searched after capture. The Nazis viewed blacks, Slavs, Jews, gypsies and other ethnic groups as sub-human.

mander immediately ordered the gun embrasure East to fire across the fort to eliminate the white flag. Half a dozen rounds swept the flag away. The gesture was futile, however; within minutes American troops had thrust demolition charges through the embrasure. The rear doors of the bunker flew open and half a dozen dazed and wounded reservists staggered out. Inside lay a dozen dead comrades. Desertion was never an easy, or risk free, option.

Mutiny

Even rarer than desertion, was mutiny: collective disobedience of orders and authority. Only a handful of German soldiers were executed for mutiny during World War II. Most of the few mutinies that did occur were among foreign volunteer troops. Such mutinies were usually the result of Nazi racism and insensitivity to the cultural and religious needs of non-German troops. Typical of such incidents was the mutiny that broke out amid the SS Eastern Turkish Volunteer Formation in Slovakia over Christmas 1944. During autumn 1944, rumours ran wild through this formation of predominantly Muslim Turks that the Germans intended to incorporate them into General Vlassov's Russian National Liberation Army, a fate the Turks violently opposed. On 24 December 1944 the German SS cadre forced the Muslim volunteers to attend a Christmas Eve party. This compulsory participation in a Christian festival was too much for some of the Muslims to stomach. As their German officers and cadre got inebriated, *Waffen-Obersturmführer* (Lieutenant) Gulam 'Alim' Alimov and four Turkic NCOs led a mutiny. When a German company commander brought them gifts of cognac and cigarettes and forced the Muslims to drink the alcohol, all hell broke loose. The German officer and his orderly were murdered and a general settling of scores followed in which several dozen drunken Germans were killed. Finally, some 500 Muslim troops deserted. Some 300 subsequently returned or were rounded up, but 200 evaded detection and joined the Slovak Resistance movement. The mutiny led to another 'reorganisation' – a Nazi euphemism for purge – of the formation, but it was considered so unreliable that it never saw frontline combat.

Prisoners of war and war crimes

One of the worst blemishes on the record of the German Army during World War II was its treatment of enemy prisoners of war (POWs), which varied in direct proportion with the perceived racial standing of the prisoners. British and American POWs received, on the most part, correct treatment in accordance to the provisions of the Geneva Convention. The further one went down the Nazi racial hierarchy, the worse things got. Slavic prisoners, in particular, received appalling treatment. It was in the brutal war in Russia, where the Nazis pursued a vicious ideological war of extermination unlike any in the history of warfare, that atrocities became common, for Hitler's goal was not just the defeat of the USSR but the extirpation of Communism and the enslavement and exploitation of the Slavs.

Thus from the earliest days of the Eastern Campaign, most German formations complied with Hitler's infamous Commissar Order to execute summarily captured Soviet political officers. Behind the front, extermination squads – the *Einsatzgruppen* – frequently working in conjunction with regular Army units murdered half a million Soviet 'racial undesirables' – Jews, gypsies, intellectuals and village elders – in the first year of the war alone. During that same period, the German Army took close to four million prisoners, yet within a year three quarters of them were dead as a result of abuse, mistreatment and neglect. Since the USSR refused to sign the Geneva Convention, the Germans claimed that they had no legal obligation to adhere to the norms and rules of war. Released from these restraints and suffused with Nazi racism, German soldiers inflicted terrible cruelties against the Soviet people.

Given this behaviour, it is hardly surprising that German soldiers feared mistreatment if taken prisoner. This fear proved to be a great motivator that the German military exploited to keep troops fighting, often in hopeless situations. Nazi propaganda constantly dwelt on the 'fact' that their enemies would mutilate, torture, even racially infect, them. Such fear of 'racial' contamination sometimes proved a weapon in the hands of the Allies. On 17 August 1944, for instance, Canadian troops captured a wounded member of the 12th SS Panzer Division *Hitlerjugend*. The division had left 50 troops to hold the Falaise High School to cover the retreat of the division. The rear-guard lived up to the billing: it held out for two entire days until it was completely wiped out and only a handful of wounded survivors were taken prisoner. One Hitler Youth prisoner arrogantly refused to answer any questions under interrogation, until that is, his Canadian captors threatened to transfuse him with Jewish blood to 'help' him recover from his wounds. Straight away, the young Nazi began to talk, answering all the questions asked of him. Even the dreaded Hitler Youth had their Achilles' heel.

In the East, German fears about mistreatment if captured became a reality as Nazi brutality

Above: Royal Navy personnel, captured after the St Nazaire raid, are escorted into captivity by a large group of German soldiers.

established a vicious cycle of atrocity and reprisal in which often no quarter was offered or given. When 91,000 German troops surrendered at Stalingrad in early February 1943, they awaited a grim fate. Thousands died within days as a result of executions, savage beatings or the rapid spread of disease through unsanitary prison camps. Those that survived faced years of hardship and toil undertaking hard labour in Soviet penal Gulags. When the Soviets finally released the survivors in 1955, less than 5000 remained.

Many of those who avoided death via summary execution and untreated wounds immediately died within weeks from the bitter cold, for temperatures were often 25 degrees below zero in winter, and the first overnight halts on the march into captivity were made on the open Steppe. Here, hundreds froze to death nightly. In the following months others died of typhus and dysentery. Those who survived worked in the mines of Siberia and died from the sicknesses associated with mining dangerous minerals. Johann Radl, a gunner in an infantry division, survived Stalingrad. Radl was lucky: having survived a forced march on foot to Kholkoz on the Volga in mid-winter, he was fortunate in that his father had been a member of the illegal Communist Party of Austria who had been imprisoned by the Nazis for listening to a foreign radio station. Radl's captors checked and verified his story. With these *bona fides*, he was 're-educated' into Communism and given the task of 're-educating' his fellow German soldiers. He pursued this task so diligently that he was released in January

1945, even before the war had ended, a mark of his dedication to his new ideology.

A more grisly fate awaited those unwilling or incapable of 'rehabilitation'. A German grenadier recalled his experience of being taken captive at Stalingrad. He was forced marched through deep winter snow, and robbed of all his possessions, including his boots and medals. He remembered vividly trying to sleep in the chilling cold out on the snow-covered Steppes and of comrades dying left, right, and centre. His group of prisoners were fed raw salt fish and 'drank' from frozen ice that they smashed and crushed. Typhus, cholera, dysentery and starvation soon further decimated prisoner ranks. After 12 days, no more than 2000 German troops remained alive out of a group of 19,000. Further humiliation awaited the grenadier as he was route-marched through the ruins of Stalingrad: those who fell out of the column were bayoneted by the Red Guards. Days later, the survivors reached a proper prison camp where conditions, while grim, were superior to those that they had already experienced.

The German military bitterly complained about Soviet violations of the Geneva Convention to the International Red Cross, but largely failed to make the obvious connection that Soviet excesses were fuelled by Nazi atrocities. While Soviet treatment was indeed harsh and brutal, the Germans got off lightly, given the terrible German treatment of Soviet POWs. A bitter cycle of atrocity and revenge emerged that characterised much of the war on the Eastern Front. Only between 1942 and 1943 did German treatment of Soviet POWs improve as Germans desperately sought to mobilise anti-Communist and anti-Russian sentiment to aid their war effort. That more than one million Soviet citizens signed up to serve in the German military not only testifies to the depth of anti-Communist and anti-Russian sentiment, but also speaks volumes about the horrors of being a German POW which drove many to accept any alternative.

In the last year of the war, the Germans reaped what they had sown as the Red Army crossed into eastern Germany and visited on the Germans the brutality to which the Germans had

subjected the Soviet people. The result was violence on an unprecedented scale, when Red Army troops murdered tens of thousands of civilians and raped large numbers of German women. Ultimately the Soviet High Command clamped down on this excess – though of course it was impossible to stop – because it undermined army discipline, and stiffened German resistance.

During spring 1945, it became evident to the most myopic Nazi fanatic that the war was lost. Recognition of impending defeat spurred one last orgy of nihilistic violence as the Nazi regime and

Right: A dejected group of German paratroops captured by the Americans during the taking of Brest, a port in the Brittany peninsula, late in the summer of 1944, as the Allies broke out of the Normandy beachhead. These prisoners of war are being transported to a temporary holding area, before transportation back to England. The treatment of prisoners by both sides in the west, in sharp contrast to what happened on the Eastern Front, was generally good. Conditions worsened for Allied prisoners of war in German camps as the war progressed, as food and other supplies became short. The parcels of food and cigarettes supplied by the Red Cross to prisoners were extremely welcome.

its military undertook a last great settling of scores. Thousands of perceived enemies of the state were eradicated, including the remaining members of the 20 July 1944 Bomb Plot, and attempts were made to liquidate the remaining concentration camp and prison populations.

Given this orgy of violence, the German garrison of Berlin surrendered on 2 May 1945 with great trepidation. However, overwhelmed with relief that the war was over, the Red Army behaved relatively correctly. Major Siegfried Knappe was among those who surrendered that day. As he was marched off in a POW column, Knappe was pulled out of line by a Soviet soldier who demanded his felt-lined boots. Judging that he could not survive a forced march without boots, Knappe risked the unexpected. He screamed at the Red Army soldier as if dressing down an unruly private, and it worked. The Russian snapped to attention, back ram-rod straight, allowing Knappe to melt back into the column before the soldier could recover his composure. Knappe therefore survived to write his memoirs: many of his comrades did not.

France 1940

The first experience of war for many German soldiers came on 1 September 1939 when Hitler sent his armies into Poland. In a lightning four-week campaign, the outnumbered Polish Army fought bravely but could not stem the tide of German *Blitzkrieg*. Even before the last Polish resistance had been crushed, Hitler turned his attention to an attack on France. To the astonishment of his generals, on 27 September he ordered them to prepare for an attack on France at the earliest possible opportunity. Of course, to the ordinary German soldiers still flushed with their first victory, another campaign against the West seemed a remote possibility. But throughout the winter of 1939 and into the spring of 1940, the German Army trained hard for the next campaign which began to seem more and more likely. As April 1940 arrived, the German infantry trained hard with long marches, river assaults and night attacks, while the tanks practised their attack formations and road discipline.

The original German plan for an attack on France – *Fall Gelb* – was unimaginative and envisaged a thrust through Holland and central Belgium to avoid the powerful French defences of the Maginot Line. However, *Generalleutnant* (Lieutenant-General) Erich von Manstein managed to persuade Hitler to mount a much bolder stroke. While Army Group B advanced into Holland and central Belgium, thus occupying the attention of the Allies, Army Group A, with seven of the 10 panzer divisions available, would push

Left: Major-General Erwin Rommel watches men of the 7th Panzer Division practising river crossing on the Moselle shortly before the invasion

through the heavily wooded and hilly Ardennes region and cross the River Meuse at Sedan. This unexpected blow would, it was hoped, cut the Allied armies in two and lead to a decisive victory. Nonetheless, most German soldiers did not know the timing or direction of the next offensive until the eve of the attack on 9 May 1940. The orders to move came as a complete surprise to wireless *Unteroffizier* (Sergeant) Werner Flack, who had fought in Poland. He had hoped to get a day's pass to go to Bingen-am-Rhein so that he could enjoy the lovely spring weather. Suddenly, his *Feldwebel* (Colour Sergeant) told him to be ready to move: the company was to be on the road in four hours time. At first, he suspected that the orders simply meant there was to be yet another exercise, but once he reached his wireless office and read a slip with the unit's action frequencies on it, he knew that, this time, the orders were for real. Flack forgot about the beautiful weather, and readied himself for war. *Hauptmann* (Captain) Graf von Kielmansegge, a staff officer with the HQ of the 1st Panzer Division, saw looks of surprise on the division's officers when they received the news at lunchtime on 9 May. Many officers were still on leave and the division formed up and started its march without them. The division drove through the night, without lights, along winding roads in the darkness. With the roads filled with marching troops, wagons and lorries, the drivers had to strain their eyes to avoid ploughing into columns of marching troops or ending up in the roadside ditches.

The next day, in the early morning of the 10th, 1st Panzer Division – part of Guderian's XIX Panzer Corps – approached Luxembourg. *Feldwebel* (Colour Sergeant) Schwappacher of the *Grossdeutschland* Regiment, also part of Guderian's Corps, saw the last houses of the German frontier fade into the early morning fog. Although the Luxembourg police attempted to blow the bridge over the Sauer, the German engineers were able to quickly repair the bridge and the advance continued. Driving through Luxembourg, Schwappacher was astonished to see farmers ploughing their fields and hardly bothering to look up as the enormous column of

German tanks and vehicles roared past. The Germans had achieved complete surprise. As the Allies moved their best armies into central Belgium to counter what they saw as the main threat, the deadly thrust of the German panzers through the Ardennes went unnoticed.

As the Germans advanced through the wooded Ardennes, they met with limited resistance, although both the Belgians and French troops skilfully demolished most of the bridges in the path of the German advance. A *Pionier Leutnant* (Second Lieutenant), Karl Heinz Mende, was amazed at the speed and smoothness of the advance. It seemed to him that the German advance was simply swamping the Belgian resistance and that the whole campaign was like a sand table exercise rather than war. By the evening of 12 May, just two days after the campaign began, the spearheads of the 1st Panzer Division had reached the Meuse at Sedan. Further north, Reinhardt's XLI Corps was also reaching the Meuse. *Unteroffizier* (Sergeant) Sievert, a member of a storm troop detachment with 6th Panzer Division, was unnerved by the silence and inactivity on the French bank. It seemed that either the French had collapsed and had no idea that the Germans had reached the Meuse, or that they were preparing a hellish reception for the invaders.

Across the Meuse

At Dinant, to the north of Monthermé, Rommel's men of the 7th Panzer Division were discovering just how unprepared the French really were. Foot patrols from the divisional motorcycle battalion had discovered an intact old weir which stretched across the river. Once it was dark, *Oberst* (Colonel) Furst quickly ordered his men to cross using the weir and to gain a foothold on the French bank. He watched as his men rushed out of the tree line towards the weir. French star shells lit up the scene as his men froze before groping their way in the renewed darkness down to the river. With machine-gun sections giving covering fire, the first group of troops balanced like tightrope walkers as they crossed the weir. Even though, once across, these soldiers were

Above: Troops of a German infantry section man an MG 34 machine gun set up on the top of some entrance steps in France 1940.

pinned down by French machine-gun fire, this group was reinforced slowly until several companics were across the river, and no attempt was made to dislodge them. Furst's daring and his soldiers' bravery had been well rewarded.

The next day, 13 May 1940, represented the critical moment in the entire campaign. As the German spearheads made their preparations to cross the River Meuse, the French commanders opposite them were still unsure as to whether this was the main blow. At 0300 hours that morning, Rommel drove down to Dinant to discover what was happening. He found that the men of his 6th Rifle Regiment were preparing to cross the river in rubber assault boats to reinforce the beleaguered motorcycle battalion. But the French had woken up to the danger and poured artillery

and machine-gun fire into the area. The first attempts to cross had failed with heavy casualties. *Hauptmann* (Captain) König of the 25th Panzer Regiment was ordered to bring his tanks up to the river in order to support the infantry's attempts to cross. As he approached the Meuse, he found a terrible situation. Half of his tanks did not reach the Meuse as they threw tracks or broke down, and those that did reach the river were confronted with numerous French bunkers. Many of the houses on the other bank were also prepared for a stern defence. The French poured a storm of fire at the German positions and the river was constantly whipped by artillery and mortar explosions. Driving slowly along the river bank, the crews of König's tanks traversed their turrets and fired their 75mm and 20mm cannon into the French positions. This German tank support began to suppress the French defenders, but even with this help, many of the German assault boats were torn to shreds by the French fire. One of König's tank crews recollected that during the attack, Rommel was ever present, encouraging his nervous infantrymen and crossing the Meuse himself more than once to direct the troops on the French bank. With Rommel's inspirational leadership, his men had crossed the Meuse and carved out a strong bridgehead in the face of punishing French resistance.

Unteroffizier (Sergeant) Prümers, a member of a signals unit in 1st Panzer Division, experienced real difficulties in the German night march to the Meuse at Sedan on 12 May. Under strict radio silence, his truck lost contact with the rest of the convoy and found every route filled with vehicles. After wandering about in the darkness for the rest of the night, he finally found his Rifle Brigade HQ in the morning. As he waited for orders, the French artillery began to fire and seemed to target every single vehicle, even motorcycles. But although French fire was periodically heavy, Prümers then witnessed the awesome power of the *Luftwaffe* in the skies above Sedan as Stukas began to bomb the town. He watched as squadron after squadron rose in the air, and then the first aircraft began their near-vertical descent, followed by the others. One after

Left: The crew of an armoured car belonging to the reconnaissance battalion of a panzer division pore over a map in France during the campaign. Armoured cars were used as the eyes and ears of the panzer division, probing far ahead of the main formation, looking for weaknesses in the enemy defences. The berets worn by these men and all panzer crews were specially padded to protect their heads when the vehicle was moving at speed or over difficult ground.

another, the Stukas released their bombs on to the French bunkers and he watched the bombs drop onto their targets. However, Prümers could not distinguish the different sounds of the Stukas' sirens, the bombs' whistle while in flight, or their subsequent detonation; instead they all merged in a deafening crescendo of overwhelming noise. Prümers felt hypnotised by the constant rising and falling of new waves of Stukas in the skies above, and he felt his confidence return when he noticed that the French artillery had stopped firing. Eventually the whole of the west bank of the Meuse was wreathed in smoke and it seemed impossible to him that any of the defenders could have survived such a bombardment.

The German anti-tank and flak gunners, tank crews and infantry all took the opportunity to move down to the banks of the Meuse at 1500 hours and pour fire into the French bunkers. Nonetheless, when the time came for the infantry and assault engineers to climb into their rubber boats and motorised assault boats, French resistance seemed to spring back to life. *Unteroffizier*

(Sergeant) Schulze of the 69th Rifle Regiment, one of 10th Panzer Division's units, found that many of the French guns opposite his unit were untouched. His unit had to cross a large meadow to get down to the river. As they crossed the meadow, the French opened fire with machine guns and artillery, which prevented Schulze and his men from getting forward. Any movement brought heavy French fire. Pinned to the spot, he could only watch as another group of *Landsers* dashed forwards and leaped into their assault boat. Another two boats followed, but the last was smashed by artillery fire. Meanwhile, a group of 12 men managed to get across and crawl up to a French bunker to take its inhabitants prisoner. After several hours, Schulze still found himself pinned to the meadows under heavy fire, while the small group of German engineers who had crossed laid out white sheets to ensure that they were not fired on by their own side. Eventually, Schulze and his men were pulled back that night to their concentration area without having crossed the Meuse.

Feldwebel (Colour Sergeant) Rubarth, however, and his group of 16 assault engineers, attached to 10th Panzer Division, did make it across. Rubarth managed to get his small detachment of two rubber dinghies, each with an eight-man team, down to the river through the hail of French machine-gun fire. With all of the wire cutters, grenades and other engineer equipment, the dinghies sat perilously low in the water, but after jettisoning all unnecessary equipment, Rubarth's men paddled quickly across the river. They quickly dealt with the nearest French bunker and then, under heavy French artillery fire, crawled up to the next bunker, where, using hollow charges, they blew the back wall off and threw in

hand-grenades to finish off the defenders. When Rubarth raised a Swastika flag over the bunker, he was greeted by loud cheers from the German bank. But he did not stop there, moving on to another two bunkers 100m (328ft) away. While he and his men dealt with one bunker, *Obergefreiter* (Senior Corporal) Brautigam tackled the other alone. Rubarth's engineers had cracked open the line of French pillboxes.

When Rubarth returned to the crossing to bring up reinforcements and ammunition, how-

Below: German gunners, dressed in camouflaged capes to ward off heavy rain, prepare rounds, stored in their wicker cases, for firing.

ever, he discovered that the soldiers trying to cross were being shot up by French artillery fire and their dinghies torn to shreds. Rubarth's company commander reorganised the boat crews and made another attempt to get across. Meanwhile, Rubarth and his men drank a bottle of wine in one of the bunkers to quench the thirst engendered by their exertions. Next, the French launched a local counter-attack which Rubarth managed to beat off, but only at the price of many of his men being wounded. With fresh troops arriving, Rubarth's troops set off against the second line of French bunkers, which they also managed to penetrate. By the evening of this hard-fought day, Rubarth's team of 16 men had been reduced to just two unwounded men, with six dead and eight wounded as casualties, but they had managed to reach their objective around Wadelincourt. Rubarth was immediately awarded the Knight's Cross and a commission as a *Leutnant* (Second Lieutenant) for his outstanding action. It was only through his leadership and his troops' audacity that the 10th Panzer Division had gained a foothold across the Meuse.

The most important attack across the Meuse was that of the 1st Panzer Division at Sedan itself, spearheaded by the elite *Grossdeutschland* Regiment. *Oberleutnant* (Lieutenant) von Courbiere was impressed by the eerie stillness at Floing, just north of Sedan. The total absence of inhabitants and the silence made him wonder whether the French were just waiting until his company began to cross the river. But although the French did start firing during the crossing, von Courbiere's men were able to paddle across the river without experiencing the same storm of fire that greeted the men led by Rubarth or Schulze. Soon von Courbiere and his men had advanced 3.2km (2 miles) to the La Marfee Heights, where Stukas were still pounding the French defenders. After a brief but stiff fight, his men reached their objective near Height 247 and were delighted to find some soda-water bottles in

Right: German infantry seek shelter from heavy Allied artillery fire in a stone courtyard during the battle for Tournai.

Above: Motorcycle and sidecar teams belonging to the reconnaissance battalion of a panzer division drive through the French town of Troyes.

a nearby barn from which they drank gratefully in the heat of the warm afternoon.

With the German infantry across the Meuse, the next stage of the operation was in the hands of the engineers. *Leutnant* (Second Lieutenant) Grubnau commanded a special bridging company of engineers whose task was to build a bridge over Meuse for the panzers. Even as the infantry were still paddling across the 64m- (70yd-) wide river, Grubnau and his men had started work on their first pontoon bridge. Even though their worksite was bombed and shelled, the German engineers, stripped to the waist and without their steel helmets, worked ferociously to get the bridge across the river. Within 38 minutes they had a light ferry operating to take tanks across, and before midnight the 16-ton pontoon bridge was ready and the panzers began to rumble across to link up with the infantry.

The next day was critical for the success of the German attack. The soldiers who had won the bridgeheads at Dinant and Sedan had to cope with increasing French counter-attacks which hoped to throw them back across the river. The British and French airforces also attacked Grubnau's pontoon bridges in a desperate attempt to cut off the German bridgeheads. *Hauptmann* (Captain) Kielmansegge watched the beautiful scene of the Meuse being engulfed by the noise and explosions of these attacks. For an hour he witnessed the sweating flak gunners firing at the enemy aircraft which droned overhead while the tanks continued to roll across the bridges. French aircraft dropped out of the sky with black smoke pouring from them and Kielmansegge counted 11 downed aircraft in the time that he was a witness to the scene. The Allies lost over 90 aircraft over Sedan and failed in their attempt to take out the bridges. After heavy fighting throughout the day, the Germans had not only held off the French attacks, but also expanded their bridgeheads into dangerous salients in the French lines. Major Wenck, a staff officer, witnessed an important exchange between Guderian and Kirchner, the commander of the 1st Panzer Division. Guderian asked Kirchner whether his entire division could break out to the west, or whether a flank guard should be left facing south on the Ardennes Canal. Wenck interjected: 'Klotzen, nicht Kleckern' ('Thump them, don't tap them') – which he knew was Guderian's favourite phrase – and Guderian duly ordered a full breakout to the west.

Meanwhile, the columns of German infantry continued to march through the Ardennes to link up with the panzers at the crossings over the Meuse. *Leutnant* (Second Lieutenant) Axel von dem Busche considered the march through the Ardennes to be more of a picnic than war, particularly since his weary men had used requisitioned prams to carry their weapons on the march. All this was to change once his men reached the Meuse. In his first action across the Meuse, von dem Busche had his thumb shot off when he was throwing a grenade. With this wound, his short campaign was finished.

The dash to the coast

On 15 May 1940, the panzers broke out from their bridgeheads and began to drive across the plains of northern France. Reinhardt's men at Monthermé who had failed to cross on 13 May now got across the Meuse and raced ahead, making up for lost time. Karl von Stackelberg, following in the wake of the 6th Panzer Division, passed through a deserted Charleville with all of its houses locked up and the shops empty. Von Stackelberg saw dead horses, abandoned French trucks and wagons, steel helmets, rifles and equipment just thrown away all along the route of the 6th Panzer Division. He was amazed when a column of French troops marched past in perfect order, but with no weapons. They were going into captivity without any guard. Von

Below: German motorcycle troops, their Kar 98 rifles in their hands, take a well-earned break along the rim of a shell hole.

Stackelberg was perplexed by the complete demoralisation of the French soldiers he saw. In common with most German soldiers, he had expected the French to fight with the spirit of 1914, but the speed and success of the Meuse crossings seemed to have wrecked their morale.

However, the French Army had not entirely collapsed. South of Sedan, the *Grossdeutschland* Regiment had to fight off determined French attacks around the village of Stonne in some of the hardest fighting of the entire campaign. *Leutnant* (Second Lieutenant) Beck-Broichsitter was ordered to move his 14th Anti-tank Company up to the village at midday to support the hard-pressed infantry. As they pushed into the village, his men found deserted houses and separated German soldiers running about in disorder. Beck-Broichsitter began to realise the danger of the situation when he saw a knocked-out German tank and its dead crew lying beside it. A French tank roared past his position and he had to race

to bring up three of his 37mm anti-tank guns. In a bitter contest, the men of his company knocked out several tanks, but fresh French tanks kept appearing with French infantry which supported their armour. Beck-Broichsitter did not know how long his men could hold out, as the French fire became heavier and his company was whittled away, with many wounded men going to the rear. Eventually help arrived in the form of assault guns but French Char B1 Bis heavy tanks then appeared which were impervious to the fire of his light anti-tank guns. Beck-Broichsitter thought that he might have to order a withdrawal as the tanks' fire was killing and wounding many of his gunners. Then, as one of the French tanks lumbered across the front, *Obergefreiter* (Senior Corporal) Giesemann aimed directly at the radiator grill on the right-hand side of the tank and the vehicle burst into flames. Beck-Broichsitter ordered his men to con-

Below: Triumphant German cavalry during a victory parade on the Place de la Concorde in Paris, late June 1940.

centrate their fire on this weak point of the French heavy tanks, and soon all three of the Char B1 Bis were knocked out. Beck-Broichsitter's company had lost 12 dead and 16 men wounded but knocked out 33 French tanks. Somehow, the *Grossdeutschland* Regiment had saved the German bridgehead from disaster.

By the next day, 16 May, Guderian's panzers were out into open country and were motoring deep into the French rear. *Hauptmann* (Captain) Kielmansegge drove through countryside where everything was shot up or burnt and the smell of burning houses filled the air. The German soldiers were even ordered to milk cows that had not been milked for days, but the speed of the advance soon made this impossible. On 17 May, although Guderian was furious with the halt order which was imposed on him by Hitler and von Rundstedt, his troops were glad of the day's rest. It was the first opportunity for the exhausted soldiers to catch up on sleep and for the panzer crews to maintain their tanks and vehicles.

On 20 May, Guderian's troops entered Amiens with their proud commander, there to witness the

capture of this historic city. The 2nd Panzer Division, after refuelling, pushed on to Abbeville. The Germans had now reached the coast and cut off the northern Allied armies. That night, Guderian sent a message to his corps: 'Today's battles have brought us complete success. Along the whole front the enemy is in retreat in a manner that at times approaches rout.' But Rommel's 7th Panzer Division had a very different experience the next day at Arras, when they were attacked by the 58 British Matilda tanks of 'Frankforce'. The newly arrived troops of the SS *Totenkopf* Division were shocked to find that their anti-tank guns could not penetrate the thick armour of the British Matilda tanks, and the German gunners abandoned their first defensive positions in panic. Rommel himself found it an 'extremely tight spot'. The German infantry, one *Landser* vividly recalled, were retreating in disorder, followed by the anti-tank crews and even some artillerymen, as the British tanks rumbled forwards and dealt with the defending German tanks. Eventually, by running from gun to gun, Rommel brought his artillery pieces and 88mm flak guns into action against the British tanks which began to withdraw after a number had been knocked out. This small counter-attack by a limited British force caused more concern to Rommel and the German High Command than any other Allied action, but it was far too small to turn the tide in the Allies' favour.

Although there was fierce fighting around Boulogne and Calais during 22–24 May, Hitler ordered his panzers to halt on the line of the Aa canal on 24 May. While this gave the troops a much needed rest, it also gave the British Expeditionary Force (BEF) time to organise the Dunkirk perimeter and prepare its escape to Britain. When the Führer's halt order was rescinded, the German soldiers pushed their way into a shattered Dunkirk, but the bulk of the BEF had already gone. With the northern Allied armies crushed, Hitler and his generals turned their attention to the rest of France.

On 5 June 1940, the Germans attacked the Weygand Line, the French defensive positions which had been hurriedly prepared south of the Somme. The French infantry and gunners, hopelessly outnumbered but deployed in tough hedgehog positions throughout the countryside, fought with desperate courage. Von Stackelberg noted that the French fought to the last man amongst the ruined villages along the Somme and that some of the hedgehog positions continued to fight when the Germans had advanced over 32km (20 miles) behind them. Even with this desperate resistance, after two days of heavy fighting, the panzers broke out into open country and began to fan out across France. On 11 June, the French authorities declared Paris an open city, which struck a mortal blow at the remnants of French morale. On 14 June, *Oberstleutnant* (Lieutenant-Colonel) Dr Hans Speidel met with two French officers who delivered the city to him. Under clouds and rain showers, the weary but elated *Landsers* of the 87th Infantry Division entered Paris without firing a shot. Although French units still mounted a scattered resistance, it was clear that France could not continue. On 22 June 1940, the French Government signed an armistice with Germany in the same railway carriage where, 20 years earlier, the Germans had been forced to admit their defeat in World War I.

After the armistice had completed France's humiliation, von Stackelberg was amazed at how quickly the French settled down to their ordinary rhythms of life. He watched a family in Lyons take over half an hour to decide their lunch menu and then spend the rest of the meal discussing local gossip just one day after the Armistice. In Paris, the German troops began to enjoy the fruits of victory by going to the Moulin Rouge, buying souvenirs and risqué postcards, and settling down as an occupation force. The final *Wehrmacht* communiqué of the campaign was transmitted on 25 June 1940: 'There are no Allies any more. There remains only one enemy: England.' The German soldiers, flushed with their astonishing victory, were sure that the war would soon be over. But during the next nine months these *Landsers* and panzer crews were soon to discover that their Führer now wanted them to fight both the British in North Africa as well as the Bolsheviks in the East.

North Africa 1941–43

Rommel's 'Afrika' *Korps* was a unique formation in the *Wehrmacht*. Neither the German High Command nor Hitler had any plans to create a force to fight in North Africa before 1940. It was only the failure of Mussolini's 'parallel war' in North Africa and the imminent capture of the Italian colony of Libya which forced Hitler to dispatch a small force to Tripoli – under the command of *Generalleutnant* (Lieutenant-General) Erwin Rommel – to bolster his shaky Italian Allies. The *Afrika Korps* was born unexpectedly, but became one of the most famous formations of the German Army. On its formation, the *Deutchses Afrika Korps* was composed of the 5th Light Division and the 15th Panzer Division. On 1 October 1941, 5th Light was strengthened and retitled 21st Panzer Division. These two divisions were joined in August 1941 by the 90th Light Division, which was known as the *Afrika Division*. Although the Axis Army in North Africa became the *Panzerarmee Afrika* in January 1942, the three divisions of the *Afrika Korps* remained the heart and the striking power of the formation.

Relations between the *Afrika Korps* and their Italian allies in the desert were often uneasy. The Germans possessed that natural arrogance which comes from victory, while the Italians struggled with an inferiority complex after their crushing defeat in February 1941. The German

Left: The crew of a heavy anti-aircraft gun fire it in the anti-tank role against British armour in North Africa.

soldiers were often amazed at the structure of the Italian Army. One *Landser* recalled that Italian officers lived lives of luxury, with good food and even a mobile brothel which moved about the desert in a large caravan. The Italian soldiers ate after the officers and on a much poorer scale of rations. While the German soldiers were used to their officers leading them in battle, Italian officers generally did not leave their bunkers, leaving their men to do the fighting. Thus there was a lack of understanding between the allies which was never fully bridged. *Obergefreiter* (Senior Corporal) Hans Schilling noted that most German soldiers did not look on the Italians as disciplined soldiers like themselves, but did not blame the Italian soldiers, since their officers did not concern themselves with their welfare.

Due to their service far from Germany in the harsh conditions of the desert, the men of the *Afrika Korps* developed a very special brotherhood which bonded them and gave them a sense of identity. *Leutnant* (Second Lieutenant) Ralph Ringler remembered that when he heard that he had been accepted for the *Afrika Korps*, he jumped around like a madman and hugged the other 'lucky ones'. He could not believe that he was really going to Africa and noted that immediately he became part of a separate caste in the barracks. He had become one of 'the Africans'.

Even the voyage from their camps in Germany to North Africa was far more of an adventure than the standard railway transport that took men to the Eastern Front. *Kanonier* (Bombardier) Werner Susek of the 190th Artillery Regiment had a typical experience in reaching North Africa from Germany. He left Wahn, near Cologne, on 27 April 1941 and stayed at Bagnoli near Naples for some weeks. His regiment embarked on two troop transports which sailed for Benghazi, but two days out, they were attacked by British bombers. This caused no damage, but his transport developed engine difficulties and had to stop at Crete for repairs. Susek finally landed at Tripoli after a long voyage and joined his unit in the desert. Almost every German and Italian troop- and supply ship sailing for Tripoli or Benghazi had to run the gaunt-

let of British aircraft and submarines based at Malta. Only in early 1942 with Kesselring's attempt to neutralise Malta from the air did the Axis merchant ships cross freely. Malta's action as a thorn in the side of Rommel's supply line would eventually strangle the *Afrika Korps*.

There was another way to reach Africa. Many contingents of German troops were flown into Tripoli or Benghazi by the *Luftwaffe*. *Gefreiter* (Lance-Corporal) Karl Susenberger, a reinforcement for the 104th Panzer Grenadier Regiment, flew from Brindisi in southern Italy in April 1942. The men were divided into groups of 18 and then handed life-jackets and bundled onto the waiting Junkers JU-52 aircraft. Sitting in a window seat, Susenberger watched the flight of 35 JU-52s as they taxied on the runway, and he was thrilled to see the aircraft in the air. The aircraft landed at Crete and Susenberger had to wait four days before the convoy set off for Africa with a puny fighter escort of two ME110s. As they neared the African coast, British fighters bounced the convoy and shot down three of the JU-52s filled with German soldiers. Air transport to Africa was a hazardous business.

Rommel reached Tripoli on 12 February 1941, two days before the advance party of the 5th Light Division arrived. His orders were clear: he was to use his *Sperrverband* (blocking force) defensively to shore up the Italian forces and prevent the British from capturing Libya. However, Rommel had other ideas, and his new troops were eager to be launched into an offensive. *Oberleutnant* (Lieutenant) Wolfgang Everth commanded an armoured car company in the 5th Light Armoured Reconnaissance Battalion during one of their very first recce missions. Early on the morning of 28 February 1941, he spotted two British armoured cars advancing. They moved slowly, often halting for better observation. When they were 600m (656yds) away, two men got out of the British vehicles and advanced slowly on foot. When the British armoured cars were exactly opposite his men, he gave the word to open fire, but although several shots from his 20mm cannons hit the second armoured car, none of the anti-tank guns managed to score a hit because

Above: Troops of the Afrika Korps *drag boxes of ammunition across the sand to an anti-tank position based around a 5cm Pak 38 gun.*

the weapons were firing new 'tropical ammunition' and had not been adjusted. The British armoured cars sped off, chased by Everth's eight-wheeler armoured cars, but after a high-speed pursuit of 6km (3.7 miles), the British cars managed to escape. Everth's men later picked up the British Lieutenant and NCO who had made off on foot. After this eventful brush with the British, Everth and his men drove back 150km (93.2 miles) to their battalion area where they were filmed by a German propaganda team.

These first skirmishes tested the mettle of the newly arrived German troops and gave them valuable experience in coping with the desert conditions. In fact, most of the soldiers who

formed the first units of the *Afrika Korps* were completely unprepared for the conditions in the desert. *Gefreiter* (Lance-Corporal) Hans Schilling remembered that there were a number of former French Foreign Legion soldiers in his 1st Company, 200th Infantry Regiment. The most stubborn was Otto Kindereith who always replied to an order 'Oui, mon capitaine.' Even though his officer ordered him to speak properly, his reply was always the same: 'Oui, mon capitaine.' Although the Foreign Legion veterans knew the desert, the majority of German soldiers found North Africa to be very different from the dreams of tropical nights, palm trees, sea breezes and oases that had made many volunteer.

Adapting to the desert

Even their equipment and uniforms had to be designed very rapidly and much of it proved inappropriate. *Schütze* (Private) Charles Hintze remembered that the official 'tropical' uniform of long lace-up canvas boots, breeches, uniform coat in olive green and pith helmet was soon discarded by most Africa veterans, and replaced with soft shoes, short socks, shorts, shirt and a soft, long-peaked field cap. This comfortable and practical uniform became the distinctive trademark of the *Afrika Korps*. Their weaponry was, of course, standard *Wehrmacht* issue, although the tanks had to be fitted with 'tropical' filters to cope with the desert conditions. Another problem was camouflage and an appropriate colour scheme for their vehicles. The first vehicles were painted in standard field grey as the quartermaster department had no suitable paint. The first expedient was to cover the vehicle in oil and then throw sand on top. Soon, however, vehicles were being painted in a much more suitable desert yellow.

Nonetheless, *Gefreiter* (Lance-Corporal) Dieter Hellriegel, like many German drivers, preferred Italian or captured British trucks since they were more suited to the desert conditions. The German Opel and Mercedes trucks had double rear wheels which tended to trap rocks between them and puncture. Hellriegel was constantly scrounging for British trucks which had proper 'sand tyres'. Another problem initially was the fact that the standard German Army field kitchens and bakeries were useless, as they were wood fired in an area with virtually no trees! All the wood had to be transported over from Italy.

Just as the men had to adapt their uniforms and equipment to the desert, so, too, they had to

Below: German soldiers inspect the wreckage of a British Wellington bomber that has been downed by one of their anti-aircraft guns.

adjust to the harsh conditions. During the day, the intense heat and haze – combined with the vast quantities of dust thrown up by vehicles – made life uncomfortable, but with sunset, the temperature dropped rapidly and soldiers then needed greatcoats. *Oberleutnant* (Lieutenant) Wolfgang Everth quickly discovered that the desert was not always roasting hot. In January 1942, he complained that he needed three blankets to cope with the cold at night and still felt like a naked ski instructor.

Sandstorms

Sandstorms could make life intolerable. The hot winds sped across the desert at high speed, throwing vast amounts of sand into the air, which reduced visibility to zero. It was impossible to stay outside in a sandstorm and some storms lasted for days, stopping all movement. Perhaps worst of all were the clouds of flies which followed the army everywhere. Whether the men were eating or drinking, the flies would be ever present.

The soldiers also had to get used to a very meagre water ration. Water was hard to come by in the desert and most of the water used by the *Afrika Korps* was desalinated or heavily laced with chemicals. The brackish taste was a distinctive feature of life. Learning how to eat, drink and wash with only limited amounts of water took real skill. *Leutnant* (Second Lieutenant) Ralph Ringler described his joy when a water truck turned up unexpectedly at his unit, the first water for days. Each man received four litres of brackish, rusty, petrol-tainted water but was overjoyed by this bounty in the middle of the desert. Ringler himself took a long drink then washed his face, saved half a litre for shaving, and then washed himself all over without spilling a drop. He then washed his clothes, shirt and socks in the thick, murky liquid that was left. Not a drop was wasted. British Eighth Army men washed their clothes in petrol but such profligacy was unthinkable in Rommel's army.

The rations of the *Afrika Korps* were another problem. While the British could supplement their rations with the resources of their Egyptian base, all of the *Afrika Korps'* food had to be trans-

ported from Italy and Germany. The real problem was that German rations were not designed for the desert. Potatoes – the staple food of the German soldier – and fresh bread were not transported as it was believed that they would go mouldy in the desert climate. This meant that the *Afrika Korps* subsisted on black bread in a carton, a little olive oil and Italian tinned meat. This canned meat, stamped 'AM' for *Administrazione Militaire*, was given a new name by Rommel himself. When he was inspecting positions around Halfaya Pass, Rommel came upon a soldier who was spearing little pieces of meat out of a tin with his bayonet while warding off clouds of flies at the same time. Rommel asked him 'How does the old man taste? And the soldier replied 'Thank you, Herr General, but I thought I was eating an old mule!' After this exchange, the Italian tinned meat was always known as 'Alter Mann' (Old Man) or 'Alter Maulesel' (Old Mule). For the first four months in Africa, the *Afrika Korps* received no fresh fruit or vegetables at all. The only vegetables ever issued were dehydrated ones. This restricted diet, with no variety and the lack of fresh fruit and vegetables to provide vitamin C, meant that many soldiers went down with jaundice and dysentery. Any opportunity to taste captured British rations was greeted with delight. German soldiers like *Schütze* (Private) Hans von Esebeck longed to capture British field bakeries and eat the fresh, white bread they produced. After the capture of Tobruk in 1942, the *Afrika Korps* lived off 'Imperial Tinned Peaches', fresh, white bread and bottles of British beer for days!

As soon as Rommel felt ready, he decided to ignore his orders and planned an offensive against the British. The *Afrika Korps* attacked the British 2nd Armoured Division at El Agheila on 31 March 1941, long before the British expected any real trouble from the Germans. Surprised by the speed and ferocity of the German attack, the British were soon in full retreat.

Soldiers on both sides were often captured by driving up to a mistakenly identified vehicle in the vastness of the desert but, on 6 April 1941, *Feldwebel* (Colour Sergeant) 'Kuttel' Borchardt, commander of the 1st Company, 8th Machine

Gun Battalion had a unique experience. As his motorcycle patrol scouted territory south of Derna, they came upon a British staff car travelling unescorted in the desert. The British co-driver opened fire, killing one of Borchardt's men, but after a burst of machine-gun fire which killed the British driver, the two red-tabbed officers in the back put their hands up. Borchardt had just captured Lieutenant Generals Neame and O'Connor, two of Britain's finest commanders. O'Connor, the victor of Operation 'Compass' which had destroyed the Italian Tenth Army just two months before, had been driving up to the front to see the situation for himself. As he was being led away, O'Connor called Borchadt a 'brave soldier' and presented him with his expensive camera. Borchardt did not have long to enjoy his new-found fame or camera: two weeks later he was killed in an assault on Tobruk.

Throughout the desert war, both sides treated their prisoners according to the Geneva Convention and often with considerable courtesy. However, there were occasions when the nature of the desert war could lead to real discomfort for prisoners. A member of the 361st *Afrika* Regiment of the 90th Light Division remembered how his company was captured near Point 175 on 24 November 1941 by New Zealanders. They were loaded on to trucks and taken away from the battle area. However, before they were allowed to bivouac, all of their boots were removed to stop any men escaping during the night. The next morning, a German column was spotted advancing in the distance and, in the confusion, as the New Zealand transport hurriedly prepared to move off, all of the boots fell out. He had bitter memories of the hours of marching over stony ground without boots which left his and his comrades' feet bruised and bloody. Nonetheless, the stark contrast in treatment in the desert to the ferocity and bestiality of the Eastern Front led the men of the *Afrika Korps* to call their war the 'War without Hate'.

Within weeks of the start of their first offensive, Rommel's men had bounced the British out of Cyrenaica, the eastern province of Libya, and now were standing on the frontier with Egypt.

Kanonier (Bombardier) Paul Schlafer had a traumatic baptism of fire in the desert. He arrived in Tripoli on 20 April 1941, the Führer's birthday. He soon found himself in the Sollum battle in June 1941 near Fort Capuzzo. This was a British attempt – Operation 'Brevity' – to relieve Tobruk. Schlafer's battery, from Panzer Artillery Regiment 33, consisted of two captured British 25-pounders and four light howitzers, and was soon under attack by British tanks. His gun knocked out two tanks, while the other guns killed more, but it was not enough and the British tanks kept advancing. When the tanks were only 50m (164ft) away, Schlafer's battery pulled out, but not before being overrun by the tanks. The battery commander, *Oberleutnant* (Lieutenant) Wild, lost a leg when a British tank had rolled over him. The next morning, Rommel flew over their position and three Panzer IV tanks arrived for support. Schlafer was astonished to learn that the British had been defeated.

Tobruk

Meanwhile, Tobruk, garrisoned by the 9th Australian Division, held out in the German rear and acted as a thorn in the *Afrika Korps'* side. *Panzer Leutnant* (Second Lieutenant) Joachim Schorm, an officer of the 5th Panzer Regiment, took part in the first assault on Tobruk on 14 April 1941. Rommel was determined to capture the important port and town of Tobruk, and he ordered the 5th Panzer Regiment, the 8th Machine Gun Battalion, and a small group of pioneers to punch through the powerful defences. At 0715 hours, Schorm and his men moved off in the bitter cold to the assault. With nerves on edge, they travelled for 10km (6.2 miles) until they reached the first anti-tank ditch around Tobruk. As the tank nose-dived into the ditch, Schorm could see the stars through his hatch, before the tank hauled its way out with its engine whining. As the darkness of night began to lift, the British gunners started to lay down heavy protective fire

Right: A grenadier checks his watch while waiting under cover with his comrades shortly before launching another attack on Tobruk.

which took a heavy toll on the men of the 8th Machine Gun Battalion. As Schorm pushed on, he found himself in the middle of a 'Witches Cauldron': well-concealed anti-tank guns firing from both flanks. With many tanks burning around him, Schorm pressed the attack and managed to knock out some of the anti-tank guns, but with his radio smashed and his tank engine playing up, he decided to retire. With many of the supporting Italian guns and 88mm guns silenced, the British tanks and anti-tank guns redoubled their fire and Schorm's tank was hit repeatedly. Finally he managed to return to camp with his last reserve of power and examine the damage. An anti-tank round had gone straight through one of his bogie wheels and pierced his auxiliary petrol tank, but although the petrol had run out, it had not ignited. Luck had smiled on the crew of Schorm's tank that day. The same was not true for the troops of the 8th Machine Gun battalion: of 500 men in the original assault, only 100

Above: Field Marshal Erwin Rommel, commander of the Afrika Korps, *emerges from his field headquarters near Benghazi in 1942.*

escaped death or capture. A subsequent attack on 1 May was also repulsed with heavy losses. Rommel and his men had not expected such a ferocious defence but they came to admire the tenacious Australian defence of Tobruk. The men of the *Afrika Korps* had to face the strain and tension of siege warfare for months and *Leutnant* (Second Lieutenant) Heinz Schmidt noted that once troops were taken out of the line at Tobruk, they quickly succumbed to illnesses and diseases that they had had to cope with during combat, and the number of men sick rose alarmingly.

The frustrating stalemate continued until November 1941, when the Eighth Army launched Operation 'Crusader' in an effort to relieve Tobruk. The British attack took Rommel and his men by surprise and the *Afrika Korps* had to fight for its life in a grinding series of battles which eventually wore its strength away. The bitterest fighting centred around Sidi Rezegh, a stretch of desert remarkable only for the tomb of a Muslim saint. A fierce tank battle raged around Sidi Rezegh for days, but 23 November 1941 stood out in the memories of *Afrika Korps* veterans as *Totensonntag* ('Bloody Sunday of the Dead'). That morning *Generalleutnant* (Lieutenant General) Cruewell formed up the panzers of the *Afrika Korps* into an enormous phalanx and drove it straight towards the British positions at Sidi Rezegh. The Italian Armoured Division 'Ariete' took post on the left, 8th Panzer Regiment with 120 tanks formed in the centre, and 5th Panzer Regiment with 40 tanks was on the right. This huge formation of tanks, half-tracks and trucks rolled forwards at 1500 hours into a storm of fire. *Leutnant* (Second Lieutenant) Heinz Schmidt remembered that the column headed straight for the British tanks. Behind a fan of vehicles of all types spread out as far as the eye could see. *Oberst* (Colonel) Zintel of 115th Panzer Regiment stood upright in his vehicle at the head of his regiment until he was killed by

machine-gun fire. One *Landser* recalled that the British were firing every artillery and anti-tank gun they had and the air seemed thick with shells. The fierce fighting lasted all day and, even at dusk, the battle still raged. The burning wrecks of hundreds of tanks, guns and vehicles littered the landscape and lit up the field of *Totensonntag*. Even though Rommel tried to panic the British into flight with his 'dash to the wire' – a raid on the Egyptian frontier – eventually the persistent British pressure and continued heavy losses forced him to admit defeat. Weary and reduced to a shadow of its former self, the *Afrika Korps* retreated with great skill all the way back to El Agheila in December 1941.

Rommel's return

Just like its commander, they bounced back with remarkable resilience and, in February 1942, pushed the British back out of Cyrenaica. Both armies paused on the Gazala line, but in May 1942, the *Afrika Korps* reached its zenith. In the battles for Gazala and Tobruk, it completely outfought the 'brave but baffled' British Eighth Army and then pursued the British in the 'race

Right: Afrika Korps troops prepare to fire their leFH 18 howitzer against enemy positions. Note the barren, open nature of the terrain, typical of the North African campaign. All the supplies for Rommel's men had to be either shipped or flown in to Libya, then driven up to the lines. As a consequence even basic supplies such as water and fuel were usually in short supply, and both sides made use of captured equipment.

for Egypt'. Exhausted, but dreaming of the pleasures of Alexandria and Cairo, its soldiers pursued the British all the way to El Alamein, just 96.5km (60 miles) from Alexandria, but there in July 1942, Auchinleck's Eighth Army finally stopped Rommel. After heavy but inconclusive fighting in July, Rommel launched his final, desperate attempt to reach the delta at the end of August. Known to the Germans as the 'six-day race', the battle of Alam Halfa finally killed any dreams of Alexandria. In October 1942, Montgomery's Eighth Army crushed the *Panzerarmee Afrika* in the Battle of El Alamein.

Forced into retreat, the men of the *Afrika Korps* fought with great skill back to Tripoli and beyond. With the Allied 'Torch' landings in Morocco and Algeria, the Axis position in Africa was untenable. The *Afrika Korps* retreated out of Libya and into Tunisia, where it joined the large German reinforcements of the 5th *Panzerarmee* under General von Arnim. Bitter at the sight of weapons, supplies and material which could have turned fighting at Alamein in their favour, the soldiers of the *Afrika Korps* were no longer unique. There were other Germans in Africa who did not share their memories of hard desert fighting. In the bitter battles at Wadi Akarit and the Mareth Line, however, they still fought with determination and professionalism. Their limited success in the Kasserine Pass in February 1942 were the last laurels that they won in Africa, as Allied strength began to tell. Eventually on 13 May, they were forced to surrender, along with all the other Axis forces in Africa. A signal transmitted to Germany on 12 May 1943, just before midnight on the eve of surrender, displayed the last defiant pride of the *Afrika Korps*: 'Ammunition shot off. Arms and equipment destroyed. In accordance with order received Afrika Korps has fought itself to the condition where it can fight no more. The German Afrika Korps must rise again. Heil Safari!' The military adventure of the ordinary German soldier in Africa was over.

Left: The crew of a British Honey light tank passes by the wreckage of a Panzer IV Model F2 'Special' with its potent long-barrelled 7.5cm gun.

The Eastern Front 1941–43

This chapter will explore the experience of the German soldier on the Eastern Front, from the June 1941 invasion of the Soviet Union to the spring 1943 battle of Kharkov, by examining five different case studies. Each of these studies gives an insight into the huge and varied conflict fought in the Soviet Union: firstly, the German soldier at the gates of Moscow in the winter of 1941 when temperatures dropped beyond minus 40 degrees Celsius and Soviet Far Eastern troops counter-attacked in the depth of winter; secondly, the war in 1942 in the mountains of the Caucasus, fought by German élite mountain infantry; thirdly, again in 1942, urban warfare and house-to-house fighting in the ruins of the city of Stalingrad; fourthly, anti-partisan operations behind-the-lines in the occupied zone of the USSR; and finally, the 'barbarisation' of the war on the Eastern Front and the involvement of German soldiers in the massacre of civilians.

The battle for Moscow

Following the attack into the Soviet Union in June 1941, codenamed Operation 'Barbarossa', German Army Group Centre pushed on towards Moscow. On 1 October 1941, with German soldiers some 80.5km (50 miles) from Moscow, the

Left: German recce troops prepare to resume their advance. The soldier on the right carries a bipod-mounted MG 34 machine gun.

Germans launched Operation 'Typhoon', their thrust to capture and push past the Soviet capital in the limited time available before winter. The German soldier had to contend with two enemies: Soviet resistance, and the weather. With regard to the weather, the Germans had an inkling of what was brewing over the Arctic Sea and would soon sweep down over the battlefield as they advanced into the USSR. As summer turned to autumn, one veteran remembered: 'The already flat rays of the sun, low in the horizon over the plains, misled us. But each evening ... ominous black clouds would build up far in the distance, towering high above the steppe. These dark masses carried in the stratosphere the rain, the ice and snow of the coming winter.' It was the weather, with snows falling unusually early on 8 October, that first delayed the German advance and made life a misery for the German soldier. Soon the snow melted and the autumn rains turned everything to mud.

During November, the mud then froze as temperatures and snow fell. The German soldiers of Army Group Centre were utterly unprepared for the approaching Russian winter since the German High Command expected the war to have been won by October. The winter equipment for the German soldier in Russia was still in Poland and had not been sent forward for fear of blocking supply lines just as the German offensive was underway. As a consequence, over their standard uniforms, the German soldier had only their denim overalls, padded with newspaper to resist the cold. The lack of shelter for the German infantry intensified the cold. The ground was frozen and so impossible for digging (except with dynamite), and local buildings had been destroyed in the fighting or burned by the retreating Soviet troops. The German 112th Infantry Division, protecting the right flank of the advance, had over 50 per cent frostbite casualties by 17 November. When the Soviets attacked the division on 18 November, not only was it depleted from frostbite, but the German soldiers found that their automatic weapons were so frozen that they could only fire single shots. As for the 37mm anti-tank guns, the 112th Division

gunners found that the packing grease for their shells had frozen and had to be scraped off with a knife before being loaded into the gun breech. Meanwhile, Soviet infantry, accustomed to the cold, attacked in quilted jackets, supported by ever increasing numbers of T34 tanks, against which the 37mm gun was useless at anything but point-blank range.

General Heinz Guderian, commanding 2nd Panzer Group, wrote back to his wife on 28 November how: 'Only he who saw the endless expanse of Russian snow during this winter of our misery, and felt the icy wind that blew across it, burying in snow every object in its path; who drove for hour after hour through that no man's land only at last to find too thin shelter, with insufficiently clothed half-starved men; and who also saw by contrast the well-fed, warmly clad and fresh Siberians, fully equipped for winter fighting; only a man who knew all that can truly judge the events which now occurred.' Yet Operation 'Typhoon' continued, with panzers and infantry still attempting to take Moscow.

On 2 December 1941, elements of the 258th Infantry Division made the deepest penetration into the Moscow suburbs, it being reported that the German soldiers could see the spires of the Kremlin. This push was the closest the Germans would get to Moscow. The weather was taking its toll on the German soldier and slowing his advance. On some parts of the front in late November and early December, temperatures fell to minus 40 degrees Celsius: the breech-blocks of rifles froze solid, oil in sumps had the consistency of tar, the drag on dynamos made starting engines impossible, battery plates became warped, engine cylinder blocks split open, and axles refused to turn. Given the over-extended position of the Germans, the Soviets launched a counter-offensive, led by Marshal Georgi Zhukov and using Siberian divisions brought from the Soviet Far East.

Zhukov's offensive began on the night of 5/6 December and employed 17 fresh armies. The Germans were woefully unprepared. Only the soldiers' grenades functioned properly in the Russian cold. To add to the misery of the cold and frostbite, many German soldiers had dysentery. Men suffering from dysentery and forced to perform bodily functions in the open risked death as a result of congelation of their anus. Meanwhile, those who could still eat watched butter being cut with a saw and the butcher's axes bounce of frozen horse meat as if it were stone. Everyday chores became impossible. If a man drawing his ration of boiling soup at the field kitchen could not find his spoon, the soup would be lukewarm in 30 seconds. Any further delay meant the soup turning cold and then frozen solid.

As the Germans fell back under Zhukov's onslaught, some resorted to self-inflicted wounds to escape the front. But with the breakdown in communications to the rear areas, this meant risking gangrene, exposure, or, if discovered, exe-

Below: The men of a German anti-tank team fire their rifles at retreating Soviet troops while the gunner mans his 5cm Pak 38 gun.

cution: self-inflicted wounds were a capital offence. To escape the horrors of the battlefield, some soldiers even committed suicide with a grenade held to the chest. Considering the cold, German soldiers called the campaign medal struck for this first winter campaign the 'Order of the Frozen Meat'.

Under the strain of the Soviet counter-offensive, panzer crews were forced to fight in the same way as infantry, as the cold immobilised their tanks. The few roads west were clogged with retreating German columns. By Christmas of 1941, Guderian had fewer than 40 serviceable tanks in his command. Among the infantry, the freezing weather caused 14,357 frostbite amputations: an entire divisional complement. Meanwhile, 'moderate' frostbite totally incapacitated a further 62,000 soldiers and slight frostbite kept many more out of the line for a few days' rest. The winter of 1941–42 was the worst for the German soldier as the German Army

Above: German motor vehicles use improvised timber decking to cross marshy ground during Operation 'Barbarossa'.

High Command was unprepared for war in the Russian winter. Subsequently, winter clothing would be issued. But even with winter clothing, the extremes of the winters bit hard for the rest of the war. After the failure to take Moscow, the battle front stabilised. Germany now prepared for its summer offensive for 1942: a drive by Army Group South to the Caucasus Mountains, the oilfields of Baku, and the city of Stalingrad on the River Volga.

The Caucasus

In the summer offensive of 1942 into the Caucasus, the Germans employed élite mountain infantry to push into the Caucasian mountain range. These mountain troops, or *Gebirgsjäger*, had fought with distinction in the battle for Crete in 1941. They would now have the task of taking the highest peak in the Caucasus, Mount Elbrus, 5630m (18,470ft) high. The fighting in the Caucasus reflected the diversity of environments in which the German soldier fought in World War II, from the deserts of North Africa and the tun-

dra of northern Finland, to the bocage of Normandy and the high peaks of the Caucasus.

The newly formed Army Group A led the German push south into the Caucasus. The aim was to capture the Caucasian oilfields centred on Baku. Spearheading the drive were the alpine infantry of the LXXIX Alpine Corps. As they pushed into the foothills of the Caucasus, the mountain infantry were given a mixed reception by local peoples. Some, hostile to the Soviet Government, welcomed the invaders; others, as General Ewald von Kleist, the commander of First Panzer Army recalled, were not so welcoming: 'In the early stages ... I met little organised resistance. As soon as the Russian forces were by-passed, most of the troops seemed more intent to find their way back to their homes than to continue fighting. That was quite different to what happened in 1941. But when we advanced into the Caucasus the forces we met there were local troops, who fought more stubbornly because they were fighting to defend their homes. Their obstinate resistance was all the more effective because the country was so difficult.'

Kleist was right to emphasise the difficult nature of the terrain that made the evacuation of wounded mountain troops particularly troublesome. Lightly wounded did their best to stay in the line as their chances of survival if evacuated were slim. Evacuation meant a trip in stages back down mountain trails on a stretcher carried by a team of eight men who worked in relays of four. One soldier recalled that casualties with severe wounds often fell off the stretcher as the bearers stumbled over the rocky terrain; for men with broken bones and infected wounds, this meant further injuries. When the casualty finally reached a clearing station, it was often too late: gangrene and blood poisoning had set in, and he would be lucky to escape with only amputation.

Back in the line, the mountain infantry fought a war without any fixed lines. Defensive positions

in the high peaks were exiguous and patrols would penetrate far behind enemy lines. In this rough terrain, the Germans found themselves out-running their tenuous supply lines as they pushed into the Caucasus. The mountain troops were also used in the push through the mountains to the port of Tuapse that resisted capture as rough terrain and the enemy blocked the Germans. Moreover, rain and snow were delaying German attacks. At the same time, the collapse of a Romanian mountain division in the face of a Soviet counter-attack defeated Kleist's final attempt to breach the Caucasus mountains in late October 1942 near Mozdok. Eventually, the defeat at Stalingrad by early February 1943 made the German positions in the Caucasus untenable and the mountain troops fell back.

As part of their push, a mountain infantry assault team conquered the twin peaks of Elbrus.

Above: A horse-drawn German howitzer, heavily laden and well camouflaged, crosses the plains of the Soviet Union.

The climb began on 17 August and, at dawn on 21 August, a picked team of climbers began the ascent to the summit. By 1100 hours, with bad weather descending, the summit was reached and the national flag raised. Nailed into the flag staff was the mountain division insignia. This triumph was, however, shortlived: when the Soviets returned to the area in late 1942, the flag's removal was a priority and a team of climbers went up to remove the flag and thus all traces of the German presence on Eurasia's highest peak.

In early 1943 the *Gebirgsjäger* in the Caucasus were forced to beat a hasty retreat to prevent capture by the triumph of Operation 'Uranus': the Soviet encirclement of the German Sixth Army at Stalingrad, which threatened to cut off all German troops in the Caucasus. The battle for Stalingrad involved a new type of warfare: close-quarter, street-to-street fighting, quite unlike the open spaces of the steppe or the rocky heights of the Caucasus.

Below: German assault troopers cross the mighty River Dniepr in a rubber dinghy in July 1941; such crossings were common in the early years.

Stalingrad

Accompanying Army Group A's push to the Caucasus, Army Group B, headed by the Sixth Army, advanced to the city of Stalingrad. The German assault on the city began on 12 September 1942. Prior to the assault, German artillery and bombers pounded the city, turning the built-up areas to rubble. These ruins formed an ideal defence for the Soviet infantry defending the city. Before long, the German infantry bogged down in a battle to take key factories in the north of Stalingrad, the Mamayev Kurgan heights in the centre (102m (334ft)), and a large grain silo complex in the south. What originally was a secondary objective now sucked over 20 divisions – including several panzer divisions – into a battle that ill-suited the Germans' chief tactical advantage: their superior mobility. The fighting became incredibly intense. German battalions were reduced to company-sized units and the triumphalist mood of the advance on Stalingrad soon evaporated. Soviet snipers were a particular problem, one soldier recalled. Taking advantage of the rubble, the sharp-shooters' favourite targets were German officers. Soon units were commanded by surviving lieutenants or senior NCOs. Everything was different in the battle for Stalingrad. Artillery fire meant not just the shell-burst but the collapse of tall buildings and falling masonry. With the constant dust of battle, the midday sun spread a ghostly light across the city and soldiers lost all sense of time.

The German soldiers particularly hated fighting in Stalingrad. The struggle broke all rules of conventional warfare and put the technologically superior Germans at a disadvantage. The close-quarter nature of battle was particularly costly for the over-stretched Germans. Fighting over a large warehouse on the banks of the River Volga in late September, they found themselves in the building in control of the top floor with Soviets below them and then more Germans below the Soviets. Like a layered cake, the protagonists fought between the floors of the building.

The German soldiers dubbed their war *Rattenkrieg* (rat's war) with fighting above and below ground and unexpected ambushes.

Above: German troops shiver in the bitter Soviet Winter of 1941–42 despite their greatcoats, bala-clavas and ear muffs.

Frequently, no quarter was offered or given. The ruins caused by *Luftwaffe* bombing and artillery fire turned the city into a defensive stronghold. The expedient of a mine or petrol bomb dropped under or on German tanks pushing through the narrow streets easily negated the Germans' superiority in armour. The battle for Stalingrad became a series of relentless isolated conflicts fought by German assault squads attempting to gain the west bank of the Volga. The assault squads would be six to eight strong and armed with knives, sharpened spades, sub-machine guns and grenades. Flame-throwers and combat engineers with explosive charges reinforced assault squads going into the sewers.

With winter approaching, the Sixth Army commander, General (later Field Marshal) Friedrich Paulus, knew that the remaining pockets of Russian resistance on the west bank had to be eliminated. Paulus' aim was to take the northern, industrial section of the city. To do this, the Germans used drains and underground tunnels, bypassing Russian pockets of resistance and reaching the banks of the Volga. Vicious fire fights were fought all over the northern sector, with Russian ambushes catching German infantry in enfilade. While advances were made in the north, pockets of Russian resistance held on. Daily gains were measured in feet.

The assault on the northern factory districts continued into October and the Germans realised that the area would not be easily taken. The Red October and Barrikady factories had been turned into fortresses and the struggle became a World War I-style battle fought in dense rubble. Defended as these factories were by the Soviet 308th Siberian Rifle Division, the Germans attacked them following a heavy aerial bombardment, meeting with continuous counter-attacks supported by Russian heavy artillery on the east

bank. Special combat engineers were flown in to help the German infantry. In an attack on 6 October on the Stalingrad Tractor Factory, one German battalion was wiped out when hit in open ground by a salvo of Russian Katyusha rockets. The Germans gained ground but at such a heavy cost that it wore down German offensive potential. The 94th Infantry Division, for example, was reduced to 535 effectives; the 76th Division was no longer fit for battle after a period in the line.

On 14 October 1942, the Germans launched another offensive. Every available aeroplane was used to soften up the Soviet defences. An officer from the 14th Panzer Division recalled how different the fighting was for the German tanks, which were used to the open spaces of the Russian steppe. Tanks climbed mounds of rubble and scrap, and lumbered through chaotically destroyed workshops, firing their main gun at point-blank ranges in narrow yards. Many of the tanks shook from the force of an exploding enemy mine and were easy targets for Soviet tank-busting teams. Panzers smashed into the factory complexes and battle became a confused contest between the German and Soviet infantry which were milling in the factory complexes.

German morale suffered under the intense fighting. One German corporal wrote home: 'Father, you kept telling me: "Be faithful to your standard and you'll win." You will not forget these words because the time has come for every sensible man in Germany to curse the madness of this war. It's impossible to describe what's happening here. Everyone who still possesses a head and hands, women as well as men carries on fighting.' Another soldier remarked laconically that a saying from the Gospel often passed through his thoughts: 'no stone will be left standing upon another'. Here at the front the soldier recognised that this saying had become reality.

Paulus planned a final assault to clear the remaining pockets of Russian resistance on the

Left: Heavily armed German infantry fight their way forward through the shattered remains of Stalingrad against fanatical resistance.

west bank. As temperatures fell, he sent in his men again on 11 November. Supported by fresh pioneer battalions, six infantry divisions went forward. Key buildings north of Mamayev Kurgan were taken, only to be retaken by Soviet counter-attacks. Desperate to take the city, Paulus ordered tank crews to assemble as infantry for the final push. Panzer commanders, desperate to keep their trained crews for future armoured operations, sent mechanics and support personnel instead of the highly trained crews. By mid-November, most infantry companies were down to under 50 men, with the worst casualties in experienced officers and NCOs. It was then, on 19 November, that Zhukov launched his long-planned great counter-offensive, Operation 'Uranus', on the flanks of Stalingrad that encircled the city and trapped over 200,000 men in and around Stalingrad. Reliant on what few supplies could be brought into the ever-shrinking perimeter by aircraft, the encircled German troops in Stalingrad slowly starved to death. In January and February 1943, the 90,000 troops remaining in the Stalingrad pocket surrendered. In all, by 1955, just 5000 of these troops returned home from Soviet POW camps. The German soldier had been decisively defeated and a great victory achieved for the Soviets.

Anti-partisan operations
Throughout the war in the East, there was an ongoing war between partisans and German occupation forces. The partisans were composed of local people, Soviet soldiers cut off in the great encirclement battles of 1941, and specialists flown in by Moscow. These partisans became an increasing menace to German troops and lines of communication. As a consequence, large numbers of German soldiers spent the war away from the 'front' fighting increasingly large and well-equipped bands of partisans. One such soldier was Guy Sajer, an Alsatian German who ended up in the élite *Grossdeutschland* Division. Sajer spent much of his time in anti-partisan operations. In his account of the war, *Forgotten Soldier*, Sajer recalled the cold, boredom and sudden dangers of these operations, where weeks with no

Right: To increase their mobile anti-aircraft capabilities the Germans mounted the 3.7cm Flak 36 gun on a range of half-track vehicles, such as this one travelling at speed on the Eastern Front. The Germans gradually lost superiority in the air as the war progressed, and flak units became more and more necessary companions for the panzers. Unless present in overwhelming numbers, flak guns were not particularly successful in destroying low-flying enemy aircraft, but they could be very effective in distracting a pilot and thereby ruining his aim. On the Eastern Front the Russians often used single aircraft as nuisance raiders at night, which were very difficult to shoot down.

contact would be replaced by a sudden partisan attack. Sajer's comrades suffered bitterly from exposure to the cold, and special 'warming rooms' were set up to help the men recover from anti-partisan sweeps they had to conduct in the winter months. Sajer's regimental doctor recommended an alcohol mix on cracked hands to ward off frostbite, a painful process, but necessary as a counter to frostbite.

The reaction of the Germans to the partisan threat was extremely savage. All partisans were to be shot, and army and SS commanders vied with each other in approving the toughest

responses to the partisan threat. German soldiers were ordered to execute 50–100 civilians for every German death. Captured partisans were publicly shot or hanged with placards round their necks *pour encourager les autres*. German soldiers, often on the flimsiest pretext, and with the help of local militias or Cossacks, would massacre entire villages. The 707th Infantry Division in White Russia in one month shot 10,431 alleged 'partisans'. Reprisals on this scale served only to increase recruitment for the partisan units hiding out in the forests and swamps of the region. In great anti-partisan sweeps, the Germans

hunts' on the slightest pretext, when villages were surrounded and the inhabitants forced out to be shot down. The soldiers would then loot the homes for souvenirs. One soldier wrote home enclosing a lock of hair from a Russian guerrilla girl with the comment that such partisans fight like wild cats and were subhuman. In response to such terror, the partisans exacted what revenge they could. German hospital trains were derailed and the occupants burned alive with paraffin. One German soldier in the Mogilev region recalled how a rumour reached them of hidden gold at a nearby state farm. With some comrades, the soldiers went to the farm and tore the place to pieces looking for gold. The head of the settlement begged them to wait as he could get the gold in 24 hours and if the buildings were all destroyed, the peasants would have nowhere to spend the winter. At dusk the Germans left with the orders that the gold was to be produced the following day or the entire population of the farm would be placed under arrest. A detachment of four men was left behind, commanded by a soldier called Fisher. The next day there was no word from Fisher on the radio, and so a detachment returned to the farm in armoured cars. They found the farm burned to the ground with only one building remaining. In it stood a very heavy leather box, *Gelb* (Gold) scrawled on it in white paint. On opening it, the Germans found the heads of Fisher and the three other German soldiers left behind.

Railways were a favourite target of the partisans. Defending the lines involved German troops travelling in armoured trains and manning blockhouses along the line. The everyday life of the Germans caught up in these anti-partisan operations was bleak. Roads were unsafe and vehicles had to travel in convoys with heavy machine guns mounted on trucks. Convoys were stopped by the simple expedient of trees felled across the road and then bullets were pumped into the halted convoy. Amongst the German occupation troops, an insidious demoralisation spread as a result of the attacks. In the end, the fear of partisans led dispirited German troops to carry out many acts of brutality.

deployed panzer divisions and air fleets to clear areas of partisan activities, tying down large numbers of troops. Swathes of the Pripet Marshes in White Russia were controlled by bands of partisans, forcing the Germans to send in troops to the heavily wooded and marshy wilderness to hunt them down, causing heavy casualties to the hunters.

In the occupied zones of the Soviet Union, ordinary German soldiers, motivated by the Nazi racial ideology, behaved quite differently to how they had behaved during their occupation in the West. Occupation troops would organise 'man

Barbarisation

German *Einsatzgruppen* (liquidation squads) and police units were responsible for the slaughter and enslavement of civilians in the occupied territories. In particular, the Jewish population was targeted for wholesale extermination. German soldiers were caught up in what has been described as the 'barbarisation' of war on the Eastern Front as ordinary soldiers committed atrocities against civilians in the belief that these people were racially inferior. These German troops carried out the most appalling acts of savagery because of the need to conform to their fellow soldiers acting in the context of racial war.

The behaviour of the German Army in the initial stages of 'Barbarossa' demonstrated the horrific character of this racial war of annihilation (*Vernichtungskrieg*) on the Eastern Front. Frontline troops operated under special standing orders that allowed them to shoot captured Soviet commissars, in defiance of international law and accepted standards of human behaviour. The German Army High Command offered little objection to these new orders. The Soviet POWs who fell into German hands in huge numbers following 'Barbarossa' were treated in a manner quite unlike the French, British and Belgian soldiers who were captured in 1940. They were frequently worked to death or marched until they died. Within six months of attacking the Soviet Union, over two million Soviet POWs had starved to death in freezing compounds surrounded by barbed wire on the open steppes.

SS troops committed the majority of the killings of civilians. One of the most notorious SS massacres was of 33,771 Jews at Babi Yar outside Kiev. Soon after the Germans occupied Kiev, partisans blew up the headquarters of the German Sixth Army located in the Continental Hotel in the centre of Kiev. As a 'reprisal', on 26 September 1941, the Germans posted notices ordering all Jews to report within three days for 'resettlement'. Believing the offer of resettlement, over 30,000 Jews duly appeared and were then marched to a 1.6-km (1-mile) anti-tank ditch outside the city. They were next taken in batches, stripped, and shot in the back of the neck. Some

Right: German anti-tank troops adjust the out-riggers of a 3.7cm Pak 36 gun during the spring 1943 battles for the Ukrainian city of Kharkov. These guns were ineffective against the heavier Soviet tanks with sloping armour. Anti-tank guns became increasingly larger, heavier and more cumbersome as the war progressed, in an attempt to counter the increased armour protection of the newest tanks. As a result anti-tank guns were commonly mounted on armoured chassis later in the war, making them resemble the very tanks they were designed to destroy. Note the vision slot in the gun's shield, the latter provided to give the gun aimer some protection from enemy rifle or machine gun bullets while taking aim.

were made to run a gauntlet of SS troops, being shot at as they ran. The slaughter took two days, and included some captured Soviet soldiers. The ditch was later covered in a thin layer of quicklime and earth. This was not enough, for six months later explosions were heard from Babi Yar as the gases from the decomposing bodies escaped through the earth. The Germans then set about exhuming the site and cremating the bodies to hide the atrocity.

Massacres such as Babi Yar were not the largest carried out in the occupied zone. At Odessa, some 75,000 Jews were killed by Germany's Romanian allies, assisted by local militias hostile to the Jewish population. Those Jews, gypsies, and other racial 'undesirables' who survived these initial massacres, were transported to the notorious extermination camps being built in the German-occupied territories of Eastern Europe.

The treatment of Soviet civilians, Jews and Soviet POWs on the Eastern Front besmirched the German Army. Ordinary policemen took part in mass executions; professors, lawyers and doctors commanded the *Einsatzgruppen*. While specialist liquidation squads and SS troops were responsible for the worst massacres, the ordinary German soldier on the Eastern Front behaved in a cavalier fashion with human life that cannot be excused by the exigencies of war.

Defeat in the East 1943–45

After Germany's shocking defeats over the winter and spring of 1942–43, Hitler was determined to regain the initiative with a new summer offensive – Operation 'Citadel' – intended to encircle and annihilate Soviet forces in the Kursk salient. He embarked on a major, but less ambitious, offensive with maximum concentration of armoured strength on the narrowest of fronts in order to pinch off the Kursk salient that protruded deep into German lines and to sap Soviet strength. German strategy thus reverted to attrition as Hitler sought to replicate the great encirclement victories of 1941. But although the Germans assembled a mighty concentration of armour, the operation was poorly conceived, and repeated postponement cost the element of surprise. Thus the Germans were attacking powerful Soviet forces entrenched in prepared positions echeloned in depth with large mechanised reserves at hand. The result was a bitter attritional struggle – the largest battle of World War II – that the Germans could not win.

Among those who fought at Kursk was *Oberleutnant* (Lieutenant) Artur Schütte, a tank company commander with the *Panzergrenadier* Division *Grossdeutschland* attached to the XXXXVIII Panzer Corps of *Generaloberst* (Colonel General) Hermann Hoth's Fourth Panzer Army. The corps thrust north from Belgorod toward Kursk. Initially the going was

Left: A German motorcycle and sidecar team desperately attempt to push their BMW vehicle through the appalling spring mud.

Above: German grenadiers grab some refreshment during a lull in the fighting at Kursk, July 1943. Note the Tiger tank in the background.

remarkably easy, Schütte recalled, as the division burst into the village of Sawidowk. The Soviets had deliberately abandoned the village, however, to lure the Germans out into the open. Immediately beyond the village the *Grossdeutschland* ran into minefields so dense that Schütte thought – with only slight exaggeration – that it would have been impossible to put even a medal between them. Soon, however, the division was embroiled in bitter combat that Schütte likened to the 1916 Battle of Verdun. The division thus stalled short of its first objective: the village of Ssyrzewo beyond the Pena River. Schütte remembered that he never saw the settlement more clearly than he did that first day: thereafter it disappeared in a cloud of smoke and dust. The panzer commander bitterly recalled being

ordered to hold ground that had been easily gained and then having heavy losses from artillery that had been preregistered on the abandoned terrain. Schütte complained to his commander that 'having driven Ivan out, we should have withdrawn ourselves and let him bomb the place out of existence. Then we could have moved the armour forward relatively safely.'

Many tanks fell victim to the numerous and expertly camouflaged Soviet anti-tank guns. A heavy overnight storm that flooded the Pena River added further difficulties to the advance: the cornfields flooded and Schütte's tanks bogged down in the swampy ground. His company thus struggled forward a couple of kilometres until it reached another small hamlet that the enemy promptly abandoned. But Schütte refused to fall for the same trick twice: he was not to be caught in the lure of a deserted settlement again. In disobedience of orders, he failed to occupy the hamlet but instead halted his tanks on a nearby reverse slope and awaited the Soviet barrage which came close to dusk. Once it ended at midnight his company occupied the hamlet – which had been reduced to a smoking ruin – without loss. Its thatched cottages still blazed and dust rose in huge clouds from the rubble. As dawn approached, the company attacked and caught the enemy off guard. They had believed the bombardment had inflicted heavy loss on their opponent. Since surprise was of the essence, there was no time for laborious mine-clearing and several tanks fell victims to mines.

This attack also soon bogged down as new enemy forces entered the fray. The battlefield had now taken on a desolate appearance: miles of devastated corn, dozens of destroyed tanks and dead bodies swelling obscenely in the summer heat. Schütte was shocked by the sight of a soldier caught by a shell burst as he squatted in a ditch with his trousers down. 'It seemed the ultimate humiliation,' he recalled. Later, passing through a small copse, the company commander looked up to see the face of an enemy sniper in a tree. In panic, he fired a full clip from his pistol into what turned out to be a bodiless head, which had been blown off by an artillery blast and tossed up into the tree, where it had lodged.

Only on the third day did the XXXXVIII Panzer Corps achieve a breakthrough at Ssyrzewo which allowed Schütte's armour to take the adjacent village of Berezowka. But the Soviets quickly recovered and threw the Seventh Guards Army into a counter-attack. The result was a tank engagement between 500 tanks at point-blank range as dust clouds thrown up by manoeuvring armour blanketed the battlefield. That morning Schütte had laconically commented to his gunner that 'it was a fine day for a joy ride', but by evening he was regretting his flippant optimism: they had gained no ground all afternoon and their objective – Kursk – remained as remote as the moon. Resting that evening, Schütte realised that the Soviets had learned a great deal from the Germans since 1941.

The following day, 9 July, the Soviets went over to the counter-offensive. So heavy and prolonged was the enemy's fire support that Schütte characterised it as 'a continual earthquake'. Days of saw-see battle followed and climaxed on 12 July with one last big push which subsequently become known as the 'Death Ride of the Fourth Panzer Army' as it fought what remains the largest tank battle in the history of warfare at Prokhorovka. The day was one of intense dry

Right: A camouflaged machine gunner in the prone position fires out across wire defences during twilight, somewhere on the Eastern Front. The tracer bullets he fires show clearly in the fading light. Unless accompanied by anti-tank guns or mines, such defensive positions were of little use against Soviet tanks. Note the special section of wire erected to block the enemy using the frozen river.

heat that threw up such enormous dust clouds that visibility was reduced to virtually nil. Indeed, on one occasion a German Panther and a Soviet T34 tank collided head on as they rolled through the dust. Visibility was so poor that the German armour was unable to take advantage of its superior range and optics. Schütte's company, engaged on the fringes of battle, was pushed out of Berezowka and temporarily isolated as the Soviet High Command committed the entire Fifth Tank Army to the attack. Schütte recalled that he had never seen so many Russians: 'Ivan was streaming like rats all over the battlefield.' The commitment of the Soviet strategic reserve tipped the balance at Kursk: the offensive completely stalled and the committed forces made a fighting withdrawal under intense pressure to their start lines. The *Grossdeutschland* and other divisions had been bled white. Hitler's Kursk gambit had been played and had failed.

Army Group Centre

The failure of Operation 'Citadel' marked the permanent passing of the strategic initiative to the Soviets, and from then on, the Red Army steadily pushed back the Germans and inflicted heavy losses. As the Soviets went over to the offensive across the entire front, and as German mobility dwindled, German forces increasingly suffered encirclement and defeat. It was during June 1944 that the German Army suffered its greatest debâcle as the Soviets launched Operation 'Bagration' against Army Group Centre. Within days, the Red Army had achieved operational breakthroughs. Mechanised columns raced deep into the German rear, dislocating communications and control, and encircling division after division. By the time the Soviet offensive had petered out in September, it had not only pushed the Germans out of the Soviet Union and back into occupied Poland, but no less than 26 German divisions had ceased to exist. All that remained of many were small groups of stragglers, their uniforms in tatters, who had fought their way through many miles of enemy- and partisan-infested territory, their numbers constantly dwindling, until they reached safety. Most never

made it back: they laid in makeshift roadside graves or languished in Soviet POW camps.

Among those who survived both encirclement and the harrowing retreat was Major Otto Lemm, commander of the 1st Battalion, 27th 'Fusilier' Regiment of the 12th Infantry Division. This formation had an excellent combat reputation, being one of the original pre-war divisions. It had proven itself repeatedly in both offensive and defensive operations on the northern flank of

Right: The Panther tank, first employed so unimpressively at Kursk in 1943, became the mainstay of the German defence in 1944–45. One of the best tank designs of the war, the Panther mimicked the sloping armour of its rival, the Soviet T34, and its 75mm gun was capable of knocking out most Soviet armoured vehicles. This example is behind the battle area, as its gun is being supported by a bracket which was only used when not in combat. The Soviet Union gained a numerical advantage over Germany in tanks as early as 1942, but the quality of the German panzers and their crew's training redressed the balance to some degree. Nonetheless the Germans were forced back to the Reich by weight of numbers.

the Eastern Front. On 22 June 1944 the division was deployed in the main line east of Mogilev and Major Lemm's battalion held positions behind the Pronja River. Lemm, a five-year veteran, had personally supervised the construction of an elaborate network of defensive positions: dugouts, bunkers, barbed-wire obstacles, firing pits and communications trenches. Having learned from bitter experience the power of Soviet artillery, Major Lemm lightly manned his

forward outposts, while keeping the majority of his men in the comparative safety of reinforced bunkers built on reverse slopes. Thus, when the Soviet bombardment began on 22 June, he immediately recognised it for what it was – the opening of the long-expected offensive – and ordered the evacuation of the forward observation posts.

The bulk of the Soviet artillery fire fell on the forward positions, obliterating many of them. But the Soviets had still not learned to target rear

slopes where most of the German defenders had hunkered down. The result was that the battalion suffered only two casualties. As the barrage lifted, the enemy came: the 139th Rifle Division launched an amphibious assault across the Pronja River. Lemm's men rushed back to their forward positions and poured a hail of fire on the attackers as they reached the shore. The Soviet attack collapsed amid this hail of fire and the survivors retreated back across the river. The next day, the Soviets came again under cover of a smoke barrage and this time, they succeeded in establishing a thin penetration in one of the company positions. Major Lemm personally led the battalion's reserve company – hand-picked veterans who had shown resoluteness in previous battles – in an immediate counter-attack. He charged forward, firing a sub-machine gun from the hip, while all around him grenadiers liberally threw stick grenades as the battalion mortars fired a barrage a mere 50m (164ft) ahead of the charging troops. Soon the air resounded with the clash of steel on steel as the battalion repulsed the enemy in bloody hand-to-hand combat.

Major Lemm's resolute defence came to nought, however, as both the neighbouring battalions collapsed under the weight of the Soviet attack and the 1st Battalion found its flanks hanging in the air. Lemm was forced to make a retreat, the first of many. His troops marched for three nights straight and fought each day until they could march no more and the Major was forced to call a halt. His battalion was cut off, out of contact with higher command and uncertain of where the main German line was. Every day the battalion encountered enemy reconnaissance patrols that had to be driven off. Ammunition began to run low and morale began to dwindle.

Finally on the fourth day – 25 June – elements of Lemm's 2nd Company cracked after their company commander was killed. Troops fled in panic from their positions. Recognising the seriousness of the situation, Lemm drove to the company on a motorcycle, intercepting many stragglers on the way. He made them line up in parade-ground formation and inspected them, speaking words of reassurance and comfort to every single man.

Having calmed them, he promised he would get the battalion to safety, but he could only do that if they remained disciplined. He then personally led them back into the line. The next night the battalion retreated behind the Dnepr River at Luplovo and, in the afternoon, reached the city of Mogilev. Major Lemm immediately reported to the commander of this designated fortified locality, *Generalleutnant* (Lieutenant-General) Rudolf Bammler, and placed the battalion at his disposal.

But Bammler was a green commander with only three weeks' experience on the Eastern Front who had arrived from idyllic garrison duty in Norway and had only just been appointed that very morning of 27 June to defend Mogilev at all costs and on pain of death. He thus ordered Major Lemm's troops to reinforce the garrison. But there was virtually no ammunition in the city, and Lemm realised that to stay would entail the annihilation of his battalion. The major had no intention of senselessly sacrificing his battalion. He therefore disobeyed Bammler – a potential court martial offence that carried the death penalty – but Bammler let the major go, since he knew that Mogilev must fall and quickly. The next morning, the 1st Battalion fought its way through Russian forces that were on the verge of encircling Mogilev. After a nightmarish trek, the battalion, swelled by many stragglers, fought its way westward toward the Niemann River. Partisan groups attacked repeatedly as it struggled through the dense Nalibocki Forest. These hit-and-run ambushes gradually sapped the battalion's strength and those too badly wounded to continue were left behind with a pistol and a single magazine: suicide was preferable to falling into partisan hands. As they neared the edge of the forest, the battalion encountered friendly troops. The nightmare was over: they had reached the German frontline. But Lemm had lost the bulk of his battalion during the retreat.

There was no such good fortune for General Bammler and the rest of the Mogilev garrison. Bammler's tenure as city commander lasted a little over 24 hours. By the evening of 28 June, the garrison had been compressed into the city centre. Without heavy weapons and short on

Above: Heavily armed German soldiers advance through fields, while in the background a Russian village burns.

ammunition, the situation was hopeless. The next morning Mogilev fell and Bammler became a Soviet POW. In 1946 the Soviets would execute him for alleged war crimes.

The 'East German Passion'

During spring 1945 there spread what euphemistically became known as the 'East German Passion' as the Red Army visited on German civilians the horror and brutality that Nazi excesses had inflicted on the Soviet population. Within days of the onset of the Soviet winter offensive on 12 January 1945 that burst through the Vistula Front and into East Prussia, terror gripped the land. Soviet soldiers robbed, raped and murdered their way through East Prussia, inspired in part by encouragement from the Communist writer Ilya Ehrenburg who exhorted

the Red Army to: 'Kill! Kill! ... Smash the Fascist beast in his lair.' As rumours of atrocities spread, German civilians in Pomerania, Silesia and West Prussia fled in enormous 'treks'. Some of these were overtaken by the Soviet advance and suffered terribly at their hands. One women recalled the rape of her 15-year-old daughter by 10 soldiers and her subsequent death from her wounds in hospital. Others witnessed arbitrary mass executions. Not even the elderly were spared and many women as old as 60 or 70 were raped, often to death. Many civilians fled on foot with just the clothes on their backs in bad winter conditions.

Caught up in this flight were many rear area military echelons, female auxiliaries, cooks, clerks and wounded soldiers. Among them was Paula Hallhauser, a German Air Force auxiliary, who had served on a searchlight battery. She was one of many who made a painful journey on foot in mid-winter down the narrow Frisches Nehrung sand spit that stretched across the Bay of Danzig connecting East Prussia to central

Germany. She slept at night on the frozen Baltic sea: there was no room on the narrow spit, it was so crowded. Under the sound of the ice groaning as it thawed, she tried to sleep, fearful that the ice would crack. She woke each morning to see broken holes in the ice where people had lain down the night before, as well as the bodies of those who had succumbed to hypothermia and exposure on the open ice. Russian aircraft periodically appeared, Hallhauser recalled, and dropped bombs on the ice, breaking it up and sending many civilians to their deaths. All along the spit were signs of terror: dead bodies left where they had fallen and open suitcases with personal effects scattered about. Indeed, the column advanced, surrounded on both sides by an ever-growing wall of dead bodies, broken and abandoned carts and wagons, and dead horses that the starving civilians attacked in a hunger-induced frenzy, often eating the meat raw as they trekked along. Hallhauser was one of the lucky ones and would survive the ordeal: many did not.

Last stand

In a final scrape of the manpower barrel, Germany desperately threw into battle its young and elderly men during spring 1945. Among them was *Fahnleinführer* Lothar Löwe, the 16-year-old son of an electrical engineer, who was appointed commander of a Hitler Youth tank destruction company in February 1945 that was assigned to the 3rd Fortress Anti-tank Battle Group based at Tempelhof airport, Berlin. This company had formed up at Potsdam on the outskirts of Berlin after the final closing of the Berlin schools. Löwe – considered 'old' by the 10- to 14-year-old boys he commanded – like many a young German lad, was burning with zeal to fight, and if necessary to die, for the Fatherland. His company underwent daily instruction, he recalled, on the Panzerfaust anti-tank rocket launcher, with which they were scheduled to be equipped. Due to production shortages, however,

Left: German infantry of a Volksgrenadier *unit each carry an 8.8cm Raketenpanzerbüchse 54 anti-tank projector, known as the 'Panzerschreck'.*

Above: The last scrape of the manpower barrel: from late 1944 Germany called up teenagers and pensioners to form Volksturm *(Home Guard).*

the young troops were only permitted to actually fire a Panzerfaust once a week! Thus the members of the company had each made half-a-dozen practice shots when, on 21 April 1945, they hurriedly received brand new Panzerfausts and immediately moved into defensive positions protecting the Tempelhof airport, a vital strategic asset if Berlin was to survive a siege.

At this eleventh hour, circumstances forced the Germans into desperate measures, including subterfuge, to keep troops fighting. Löwe was one of many soldiers duped by their own government. On 24 April he picked up a leaflet dropped by aircraft and ostensibly written by the Berlin garrison commander congratulating General Wenck's Twelfth Army for opening a relief corridor through to encircled Berlin. Löwe was thrilled

and rejuvenated by the news and his growing despondency disappeared. Berlin could be held, he began to believe, once again! Little did he know that the leaflets were forgeries that had been deliberately dropped over Berlin on the orders of Hans Frizsche, head of the radio department of the Nazi Propaganda Ministry, to bolster the morale of the defenders. Wenck's spearheads were nowhere near Potsdam! The trick deceived many and kept the troops fighting in what was a hopeless struggle.

By 29 April Löwe found himself defending on the Sophie-Charlotten-Strasse with a Panzerfaust and a defective Italian machine pistol that fired erratically. Many troops were equipped with a motley array of ancient or malfunctioning weapons as the last German arsenals were emptied. His 'company' had literally been reduced to one man with a wooden leg! Nevertheless, Löwe managed to hit and destroy a Soviet tank with his first shot in anger, a feat for which he instantly received the Iron Cross, Second Class. This was one of the many awards issued during the Berlin fighting, as the German High Command literally handed out medals left, right, and centre in another desperate bid to stiffen troop resolve.

Next day, however, Löwe was wounded when a mortar round landed in front of him on the Albrecht-Achilles Strasse. He had been hit by splinters in his chest, left knee and left arm. After spending the night alone and in agonising pain, he hitched a ride on a passing tank to Potsdam where his wounds were finally tended. Thereafter, he joined the desperate breakout bid by elements of the garrison. His group infiltrated through Soviet lines on 1 May but their luck ran out and in a cornfield outside Eztzen, Löwe was run to ground and captured. Exuberant at their imminent victory, his Soviet captors treated him well. His thus avoided the fate that befell many Hitler Youth members who, fighting in their brown uniforms, rather than army field grey, were shot as partisans by their captors.

In the final stages of the war, even women fought, as circumstances over-rode the conservative and traditional National Socialist attitude toward women which had prevented the Nazi war machine from fully harnessing the female sex in the national war effort. One such servicewoman was *Hauptmann* (Captain) Hilde Lemke, sometime Doctor of Philosophy and tutor of American girl students who, since the autumn of 1944, had come as part of the Labour Service Corps to replace male aircraft spotters on Berlin's flak towers. Here Lemke and her 'girls' (as she referred to them) manned the searchlights. A dedicated Nazi, Lemke still believed – despite all the evidence to the contrary – Hitler's promises that the Soviets would be defeated at the gates of Berlin. She even disobeyed an order to leave the city, for she was determined to do her bit. Lemke thus remained at the Berlin Zoo flak tower bunker. As the Soviets approached, she was finally evacuated to the German Labour Service headquarters at Grunewalde.

From here, she volunteered to go to the Reich Chancellery in downtown Berlin on 29 April to

Below: A knocked-out half-track from the 5th SS Panzer Division Wiking *stands abandoned amid the bodies and rubble of a Berlin street.*

collect Iron Crosses awarded to Labour Service personnel. After an eventful journey, she was ushered into a side entrance of the shell-pocked Chancellery building by a *Waffen-SS* Major in a spotless uniform. Lemke picked up a job lot of 100 Iron Crosses, Second Class, and 30 First Class. She then shared a glass of champagne with the SS Major. As Lemke left, she witnessed *SS-Gruppenführer* (General) Hermann Fegelein being bundled ignominiously into the Chancellery building. Fegelein had attempted to flee but Hitler had immediately noticed his absence and ordered his arrest. He would be executed by firing squad in the Chancellery garden.

Finding her headquarters had been evacuated on her return, Lemke joined a Hitler Youth company making for the Halensee bridge – it might have been Lothar Löwe's – but they soon ran into Red Army troops who blocked their progress. She grew excited at the clash of arms and, as the young Hitler Youth boys destroyed no less than five Soviet tanks, she dashed forward to observe the action at close hand. She stayed for hours, fascinated by urban combat, but the young boys were steadily pressed back by a numerically superior enemy and, recognising that she could not escape here, Lemke hitched another ride back to the Berlin Zoo flak tower bunker.

On 1 May 1945, Hilda Lemke's thoughts turned to flight as news of Hitler's death spread. She made her way to the Zoo underground station and walked through the tunnel for several miles alongside thousands of others before exiting at the *Reichssportfeld* station near Potsdam. Lemke then marched through Spandau, all the while under enemy fire, and hitched a ride in an armoured personnel carrier until the vehicle crashed into a ditch near the city allotments. She continued on foot and at nightfall found herself alone on the edges of the city. However, early on the morning of 2 May near Staaken airfield she was captured by eight Red Army soldiers. Fortunately, Lemke escaped the vicious rape that befell many women of Berlin: her captors were too overjoyed and probably also too inebriated, having heard of the garrison's intention to capitulate that day.

Surrender

German soldiers experienced capitulation on 9 May 1945 in many ways. For some, it was a formal ceremony with officers wearing gloves and carrying daggers and swords. Some units marched into captivity, unrepentant Nazis to the last. This was especially true of élite units like the SS. When the 12th SS Panzer Division *Hitlerjugend* surrendered to American forces, one *SS-Untersturmführer* (Second Lieutenant) Degenhardt recalled, every vehicle had been meticulously cleaned and polished as best as possible in the circumstances. Most soldiers, however, awaited the ignominy of being mobbed by enemy troops, who stole medals and Luger pistols, since every GI wanted a souvenir. Elsewhere, the picture was entirely different. Motley collections of filthy, beaten soldiers in tattered uniforms trudged wearily into POW camps. Many felt humiliated at their defeat by what most still considered to be 'inferior' soldiers. Many also resented the mistreatment they received, often forgetting that they had done the same, and usually far worse, to the enemy.

Some German soldiers sought to escape by fleeing to neutral countries. Some succeeded; most did not. Typical of many was Erich Kassel, a gunner who fought in the bitter retreat back to West Prussia, where he sought safety in the port of Danzig. Here Kassel and his brigade waited to be evacuated back to northern Germany. During late April he was shipped to the Hela Peninsula where he again waited for a vessel to take him home. On 7 May 1945, a small river steamer arrived, on which he and far too many others crammed aboard until the boat was almost awash. Too overburdened to make the long trip to Denmark, the ship's captain set course for Sweden. Here Kassel was interned with several thousand other Germans. In December 1945, however, Sweden handed the German internees to the Soviets, who kept them in captivity until 1955. Unlike Kassel, most did not survive.

Right: In June 1945 the Red Army celebrated its victory with a parade at which troops displayed captured Wehrmacht *standards.*

The Italian Campaign 1943–45

In July 1943, with the Axis defeated in North Africa, an Allied armada crossed the Mediterranean and invaded Sicily. Then, in September, Allied troops crossed the Straits of Messina and invaded Italy. In the same month, the Italian government surrendered and deposed Mussolini. Immediately, German forces occupied the central and northern parts of Italy, rapidly (and often brutally) disarming the Italian Army. With the Allied invasion, the stage was set for the Italian campaign: one-and-a-half years of intense fighting as the Germans retreated up the rocky Italian peninsula, falling back on fixed defensive lines such as the Hitler, Gustav and Gothic Lines. The Italian campaign showed the German soldier as a formidable and tenacious opponent in defence. To show the nature of the fighting in Italy and the experience of the German soldier, this chapter focuses on three key engagements during the campaign: the battle for the Anzio beachhead, January–May 1944; the battle of Monte Cassino, January–May 1944; and the September 1944 battle to breach the Gothic Line.

The Battle for Anzio

On 22 January 1944, 378 Allied ships landed British and American troops of the US VI Corps

Left: German paratroopers mounted on motorcycles- and sidecars, or hitching lifts on eight-wheeled armoured cars, advance along a road.

– commanded by Major-General John Lucas – behind German lines south of Rome at Anzio. The objective was to outflank the Hitler and Gustav lines and capture Rome. The initial landing was unopposed, since the concrete pillboxes defending the beaches were empty. Allied troops captured three drunken German officers on their return from a night out in Rome, flushed out a motorcyclist and shot his pillion passenger, and discovered three *Landsers* hiding in a barn. Amazingly, Lucas then did nothing with the surprise achieved. As the British leader, Winston Churchill, remembered, far from hurling a wild cat on the beaches at Anzio, instead all they landed was a stranded whale.

The German response to the Anzio landing was rapid and says much about the flexibility of *Wehrmacht* soldiers during World War II. Firstly,

Below: A battery of German 10.5cm light howitzers, positioned in surprisingly open terrain, fire on Allied troops in the Anzio beachhead.

the Germans quickly put together an extemporised force; secondly, this force fought tenaciously and successfully to contain the beachhead; thirdly, counter-attacks in February 1944 almost drove the US VI Corps back into the sea. Considering that the bulk of the German army was busy defending the main line farther south, and bearing in mind the Allied naval and air superiority, the Germans' success at Anzio says much about the small-unit cohesion and training of the Wehrmacht's soldiers that allowed men from different units to fight together so successfully.

Kesselring's response

Generalfeldmarshal (Field Marshal) Albert Kesselring, the German commander-in-chief in Italy, was told of the Anzio landings after a German corporal escaped from the Anzio area on his motorbike and informed an officer of the 200th Grenadier Regiment. This information was then passed on to headquarters. The Anzio landings convinced Kesselring that his positions

Right: German engineers lay out the safety fuse for demolition charges as they prepare to blow an Italian bridge to slow down the Allied advance. The hilly nature of the terrain in the Italian campaign meant that such bridges were vital for the Allies to move their armour quickly forward. Building a replacement bridge could take several hours, or even days.

further south on the Gustav line would be turned by armoured forces from Anzio seizing the Alban Hills south of Rome. Luckily for Kesselring, he had already formed a paratroopers' battle group from the 4th Parachute Division ready to rush to any emergency. There were also elements of the *Hermann Göring* Panzer Division resting near Anzio. This formation, raised from volunteers, had already proved itself in combat in North Africa and Sicily. These units, along with what else Kesselring could find, rushed towards Anzio.

The soldiers of *Oberleutnant* (Lieutenant) Hermann's anti-tank battery in the *Hermann Göring* Division were ready to move out within 45 minutes of receiving the alarm. The men thought they were heading south for the Monte Cassino battle, but their destination was Anzio. Allied fighter bombers ('Jabos'), harried the German gunners all the way. As one of Hermann's men recalled, the Allied fighters had acquired the art of hedge-hopping and made life extremely dangerous for the Germans. For Hermann's battery, open roads were a race with death, and speed and manoeuvrability were vital. The men of Hermann's unit fired back at the fighters with what they had available, usually just their rifles and a few light weapons. As Hermann remembered, the Allied pilots did not

have everything their way. One cheeky pilot even waved at the German troops, but on one of his subsequent return passes, the concentrated fire of Hermann's soldiers caught his aircraft in the engine: the plane dipped its left wing and plummeted to the ground, exploding in a ball of fire.

As Hermann's troops deployed towards Cisterna, they moved around during the night, firing as they went, to give the impression of a larger force. The I Parachute Corps HQ then arrived from the Gustav line and temporarily assumed command of the Anzio sector. Fortunately, the Allies' tardiness allowed the Germans the time and space to build a containing perimeter. The speed of the German build-up was impressive. Hitler now sent Kesselring a message that the line had to be held at all costs, however bitter the struggle.

The *Luftwaffe* panzer crews of the *Hermann Göring* Division, together with *panzergrenadiers* and paratroopers who had surrounded Anzio, demonstrated their capabilities and determination in the ensuing weeks. Typical of this defence was when the Germans ambushed American Rangers trying to take the town of Cisterna. While some 731m (800yds) short of the town, grenadier Hans Göhler recalled, the Germans attacked the Rangers. The Americans hit back

Above: The crew of a 7.5cm Pak 40 anti-tank gun move timbers to form the structure of a camouflaged position for their gun.

with bazookas and sticky grenades, even jumping on to German tanks and spraying the interiors with automatic fire. The fighting was savage. Tiger tanks would grind up to the edge of ditches, depress their machine guns, and obliterate the Rangers in the ditch. At the end of the battle, however, of the 1st and 3rd Ranger Battalions, only six men returned to the American lines; the 4th Ranger Battalion lost 50 per cent of its men.

In the British sectors, there was equally fierce German resistance when Irish and Scots Guards went forward on 30 January 1944. Caught in bright moonlight, both Guards battalions were badly cut up, and when reinforcements were sent, the Germans responded with tanks and rocket fire from Nebelwerfers mounted on railway flatbeds. In appalling weather, the Germans mounted a fierce defence, knowing that if they retreated the Gustav line would be turned.

As the front settled down, the Germans divided the Anzio front into four sectors, each manned by a battle group. In the west, opposite the British sector, from the mouth of the Moletta river to Vallelata ridge, there was the battle group formed from the 65th Infantry and the 4th Parachute Divisions; then along the via Anziate there were the grenadiers of the 3rd *Panzergrenadier* Division. Opposite the Americans, the Germans placed two battle groups: the 71st Infantry Division, and the *Hermann Göring* Division. Each battle group represented a disparate collection of what Kesselring could bring together for Anzio. Many men were underaged or inexperienced, Hans Göhler recalled. All in all, the hurried organisation and regrouping to make a containing perimeter represented brilliant staff work and showed the German army at its best. At night, away from the gaze of Allied fighter bombers, guns would be moved from one sector to another to give the impression of added strength.

By 1 February 1944, even though German casualties exceeded 5000, Kesselring decided to test the Allies' morale – which he thought was low – with a series of local counter-attacks as a preliminary to a major assault to push the Allies back into the sea. These local attacks suffered from Allied air superiority, but still made significant advances. In the British sector, on 3 February, *Gefreiter* (Lance-Corporal) Jürgen Dietsche recalled, his unit used a flock of sheep to clear a way through the minefield. Desperate hand-to-hand fighting followed, with the British calling up reinforcements. The line was stabilised but hundreds of British soldiers were captured. An *Unteroffizier* (Sergeant) from the German 29th Reconnaissance Battalion with a Spandau machine gun mounted on the roof of a building could not face mowing down retreating British troops. Instead he allowed them to stagger back, many wounded, to their lines. Nonetheless, these attacks also wore down the Germans: the 3 February attack cost the Germans 800 men, 300 of whom were themselves taken prisoner.

Throughout early February, Kesselring launched further attacks. Many were without preliminary bombardment to achieve surprise. Each of these attacks met with fierce Allied counter-attacks, supported by massive air and naval support, and casualties mounted. With winter rain falling, the fighting was in thick mud and freezing cold. Gunner Private Heinz Hackenbeck of the 165th Artillery Regiment manhandled his gun in the mud to meet a counter-attack. Exposed in the middle of a field, Hackenbeck's gun crew worked feverishly to shore up the gun platform with wood. Hackenbeck's gun then received a hit from two shells. Like so many Germans at Anzio, this represented the end of Hackenbeck's war. His left leg had been torn to pieces below the knee by the force of the explosion but his breeches and riding boot stopped the blood coming out too fast. After two comrades had pulled him into a trench with his left leg hanging by the sinews, Hackenbeck passed out. Just 300m (984ft) to the rear, there was an aid station, where he was given injections for the pain and sent back with a label 'Urgent Transport'. When he woke up at a field hospital, his leg had been amputated below the knee.

Morale

German morale remained high. The paratroops, in particular, were highly motivated opposition. Even when captured they were insolent and cocky. A captured paratrooper asked where the sea was because the Allies were about to be driven into it. Other German POWs talked of the Russians being the common enemy. Others were less arrogant: one prisoner-of-war was worried about whether he would be sent to Florida or

Right: A German paratrooper with distinctive airborne forces' helmet, takes aim from a damaged house window during the intense fighting for Monte Cassino. The town had been heavily fortified by the paratroopers, and hand-to-hand combat was common. Both sides had a mutual respect for each other's toughness and refusal to give in.

Canada as he much preferred the climate of Florida. Those Germans taken prisoner at Anzio ran the risk of being sunk by U-boats when being taken away from the beachhead by ship, or even of being lynched by enraged Italian villagers.

This latter fear almost became the fate of *Unteroffizier* (Sergeant) Bernhard Luy of the 147th *Panzergrenadiers*. First interrogated by an American Jew who spoke faultless German, he was searched and then put on a ship bound for Naples. At night the engines were switched off and the German POWs in the hold were told that they were lying alongside an island as the ship would not travel at night for fear of U-boats. Suddenly, Luy was awakened by a hammering noise and the sound of shouting above deck. The German POWs began to panic and shouted to be let out. Eventually a hatch door opened and a voice called 'Rauskommen, schnell, schnell.' On deck, Luy and the other POWs found the ship's crew disembarking as the vessel had run aground and was sinking. The Germans were the last off the ship, accompanied by explosions on board and a mad scramble to escape down nets thrown by their British and American captors. Of the 46 POWs, 10 were lost and many others sustained fractured limbs from jumping from the ship onto the rocks below. Later, Luy and the remaining survivors were marched through an Italian village on the island to discover villagers waiting with knives to cut their throats. The British guards fired warning shots in the air to protect the Germans. Later, Italian women refused to make a fire for the soaked Germans and so the British guards had to bring tea and biscuits, as well as wood for a fire.

On 16 February 1944, the Germans launched their major offensive to eradicate the Anzio beachhead. The Germans now had 125,000 men against 100,000 Allied, and decided on a push down the via Anziate. Prior to the assault, the Germans dropped leaflets in an attempt to demoralise the Allied infantry. The leaflets ran with titles such as 'Beachhead – Deathshead', and 'The worst is yet to come'. American GIs got leaflets with anti-Semitic messages about rich Jewish draft-dodgers seducing their girlfriends.

Spearheaded by the élite Infantry *Lehr* regiment, the German counter-attack at Anzio went in to the east of the via Anziate. Under heavy Allied defensive fire, the *Lehr* regiment broke and retreated; the *Hermann Göring* Division's attack was similarly repulsed. Only the 4th Parachute Division made any headway, managing to infiltrate almost to the Lateral Road. This breakthrough allowed further exploitation but at heavy cost. Allied bombers pounded the German positions: several German prisoners said it was easier on the Russian front. The Germans

Right: German paratroopers wearing various items of headgear shelter in the wrecked remains of a house in Cassino under the shadow of an assault gun. Note the row of stick grenades in the box mounted on the wall. In the close range hand-to-hand combat that happened frequently in Monte Cassino, hand grenades were ideally suited for clearing houses that had been fortified by the other side. Assault guns could also be used to provide close support, but ultimately the paratroopers would have to check that the enemy positions had been cleared. As at Stalingrad, cities that had been destroyed by shelling or bombing provided plenty of cover for infantrymen and snipers.

deployed heavy Tiger tanks and Goliath tracked remote-controlled tankettes. To make up numbers, the High Command distributed young German recruits around the German battalions with older, more experienced veterans for support. Eventually, the Germans achieved a maximum penetration of 6km (3.7 miles). This success spread panic in the Allied beachhead. Papers were burnt; cooks, despatch riders and clerks were given rifles and rushed to the front. The Germans continued the assault for four days before calling it off with almost 6000 casualties.

However, the determined and efficient resistance had almost wiped out the Anzio beachhead, and these attacks contained the Allied troops, leaving them isolated and beleaguered. The Allied strategic design had been reversed. Now General Clark had to renew his offensive at Monte Cassino to take the strain off the troops at Anzio, who had landed to ease the pressure on his army at Monte Cassino. With limited resources, the Germans contained the beachhead and bottled up thousands of Allied troops. This was possible due to the training and morale of the *Wehrmacht*.

Above: A rather bedraggled group of German infantry march toward the sound of gunfire to engage the Allied front line in Italy, 1944.

Monte Cassino

If one battle summed up the intensity of the Italian campaign, it would have to be that for the hilltop Benedictine abbey of Monte Cassino. The abbey dominated the German Gustav line, controlled the Liri Valley, and blocked the Allied advance on Rome. The abbey was a site of pivotal importance: four battles were fought on and around it from January to May 1944. To give some idea of what the fighting was like for the German soldiers at Monte Cassino, a 'snapshot' will be offered of the battle for the town of Cassino, scene of some of the heaviest fighting.

From February to March 1944, in the second and third battles, this town, at the foot of Monte Cassino, was the scene of bitter house-to-house

fighting. German paratroopers, many veterans of Crete, were tasked with holding the town and railway station even though Allied troops surrounded the town on the lower slopes of Monte Cassino. The fighting was intense and fluid as both sides sought to encircle the other. The Allies had superior firepower, but the Germans had been fortifying the town buildings. The paratroopers of the German 1st Parachute Division strengthened basement cellars and built underground tunnels to aid movement under fire; they turned buildings into strongpoints and established numerous machine gun and sniper posts. The battle for the town was fought largely against the 2nd New Zealand Division.

Many troops of the 1st Parachute Division recollected that their formidable and arrogant commander, *Generalmajor* (Major-General) Heidrich, tolerated no weakness and had no thought for his own comfort. In the town itself, the commander of the 3rd Parachute Regiment, *Oberst* (Colonel) Heilmann, came to represent the other prop for the paras. His courage was legendary, even extending to driving his sports car close to the battlefront while under enemy artillery observation. In Cassino town, the paratroopers dragged mattresses and sofas into the basements to make life comfortable. There they awaited the Allied attack. A huge air fleet appeared over the German positions and bombed what remained of the town into rubble. The German pioneers of the 3rd Parachute Regiment had known that an air attack was coming as the New Zealanders only 90m (100yds) away had disappeared to escape the impending bombing. The bombing was intense: cellars shook, and paratroopers clung to one another as wave after wave passed over the town. Dust filled the cellars, hampering breathing. Some paras dug holes under tanks; many found shelter in caves in the hillside below Monte Cassino; most hung on in the deepest cellars they could find. A private of *Oberleutnant* (Lieuten-

ant) Schuster's 7th Company remembered vividly that the barrage formed an 'indescribable and infernal bedlam of noise'. As with the battle of the Somme in 1916, the German soldier waited with his weapon for the bombardment to pass before rushing out to take up his position in the line.

When the New Zealanders attacked under a creeping barrage, they were amazed to be met by concentrated fire. While 75 per cent of the 3rd Parachute Regiment had been killed, the remainder put up a stiff fight. Hidden German snipers picked off the tank drivers who were attempting to negotiate the ruins of the town. One New Zealander compared Cassino town to the end of the earth. For added defence, the Germans formed 'hedgehogs', all-round defensive strongpoints. For example, in the corner of the old fishmarket, a handful of German pioneers under

Below: A mortar section operating three 8cm GW 34 weapons in the ruins of Cassino, firing from within the ruins for cover and protection.

Oberleutnant (Lieutenant) Cord turned their building into a fortress and fought a protracted struggle with the New Zealanders next door. His men threw mortar shells into the upper windows and fought room-to-room for several days.

The shortage of men forced Heilmann to call up his butchers, bakers and clerks, inspired by their colonel to risk their lives. The *esprit de corps* of the German paras in Cassino town was immense. They dug in a tank in the lobby of the Continental Hotel and mined shell holes. Maori soldiers seeking shelter in craters were blown apart by the mines. The fighting was jumbled. In the fish-market a German stretcher-bearer was taken prisoner. Angered by this breach of etiquette, the Germans hit the New Zealanders with everything they had, including anti-tank rifles.

Eventually, the New Zealanders' attack was called off. However, this meant that the wounded Allied soldiers who had been fighting for the abbey had to be brought down through the town. As Major Böhmler of the 1st Parachute Division recounted, the Germans allowed the British and Indian troops above the town to retire without hindrance. Heavily bandaged and with a prominent Red Cross flag, they made their way in small groups and in broad daylight to Castle Hill. From there they slipped through the 183-m (200-yd) gap between the Castle and Cassino. The paratroops let them pass unmolested, and Böhmler refrained from prying too closely into the nature and severity of their wounds. Here, as at Arnhem in September 1944, the Germans showed consideration towards a gallant enemy.

The abbey at Monte Cassino and Cassino town were taken by an Allied flanking operation that forced the German paras to retire. Many had to be ordered to leave; some disobeyed and remained to fight it out to the end. The ability of the German soldier to fight three battles at Monte Cassino, each time checking heavy Allied attacks, says much about the toughness of the German soldier in defence. This tenacity, together with the ability to make local counter-attacks, continued once Rome fell on 5 June 1944. The Germans fell back again, this time to a new line stretching across northern Italy: the Gothic line.

Above: A German leutenant issues orders to his machine pistol-wielding platoon NCO during the Italian campaign.

Battle for the Gothic line

The Gothic line (called by the Allies the Pisa-Rimini line) stretched from Pesaro on the Adriatic to Massa on the Mediterranean. The Gothic, like the Hitler line, made much use of gun turrets embedded in concrete and steel. Construction of the line had been delayed by the building of the Hitler and Gustav lines further south, but once these were breached the Germans worked frantically to finish the Gothic line.

The Gothic line had embedded Panther turrets, some with an 88mm gun, in steel and concrete bases. Close to the ground, these guns had extensive fields of fire while themselves being hard to hit. Surrounding the Panthers were steel shelters for infantry, rock tunnelling with carved defensive embrasures and deep minefields. The Gothic line made excellent use of the hilly terrain that lay cross-grained to the Allied advance. The effect was an obstacle zone some 16km (10 miles) deep, across which attacking Allied troops would have to pass. The Germans employed 15,000 Italian labourers to help build the line, supervised by the 'Todt' Organisation. The Germans then created a 'free fire' zone by evacuating the local population across the construction area.

The Germans manned the forward areas of the Gothic line as lightly as possible, preferring to keep reserves behind the line for rapid counterattacks. To break the Gothic line, the Allies planned to use their overwhelming firepower, coupled with a plan to attack on the Adriatic coast and in the centre in such a way that would distract and disperse the Germans. Kesselring deployed his units as best as he could. He still had the crack (if depleted) 1st and 4th Parachute Divisions, the 16th SS *Panzergrenadier* Division, and elements of the 5th *Gebirgsjäger* Division, in addition to 15 other formations. The Germans again proved themselves devastatingly adept in defence. To breach the defences, the Allies pounded the line with their considerable artillery and air power. Nevertheless, progress was slow and the German soldier made the Allies pay dearly.

The Germans made extensive use of Panzerfausts to blunt Allied armoured attacks. Tankbusting teams would stalk Allied tanks. This forced the Allies to use infantry to clear all the hedges and ditches ahead of the tanks, a lengthy process, especially as the Germans had snipers with the Panzerfaust teams to hold up the infantry. The élite alpine troops defending the Gemmano ridge proved their mettle when attacked on 4 September, *Jäger* Wilhelm Rentrop recalled. First, they engaged the British Shermans at long range with anti-tank guns. The high velocity rounds tore into the Shermans and frequently ignited their fuel. Even a glancing blow would gouge metal from the turret side. As the Shermans got closer, the Panzerfaust teams got to work. These troops would let the Allied tanks pass and fire from behind, a hazardous practice. Meanwhile, what few German tanks were available were in hull-down positions to give maximum defence and concealment. Eventually, the terrain and German resistance checked the Allied assault on Gemmano.

All through early September 1944, battles raged as the Allies sought a way through the Gothic line. Bitter fights ensued in the small towns and hills surrounding the Gothic line. As with Monte Cassino and Anzio, the German soldier, despite having little air cover and being outgunned, made the Allies pay a high price for little gain. In the villages of the area, Rentrop recalled, the Germans hid in cellars and then called in their own artillery on top of them as the Allies attacked. This devastated the attackers, while the Germans hoped to survive in their cellar strongholds. After a week's fighting, the Allies failed to break though.

Between 10–14 September, the Allies again tried to pierce the Gemmano ridge position. The mountain troops defending the ridge scrambled down to the protection of the reverse slope as the British guns pounded the top of the ridge. They then ran back into their trenches in time to set up their Spandaus when the shelling stopped and before the British infantry could reach their defences. Eventually weight of numbers began to tell and the Gothic line started to crack, Rentrop recollected. Determined attacks backed up by firepower wore down the German defenders. While the Germans could inflict more casualties, the incessant battles tested German morale. They were being pounded by artillery and air strikes and levered out of their defensive positions one by one. However, the Germans were holding out for the autumn rains that would swell the rivers of the region. Each isolated post that held out for an extra hour brought closer these rains which made movement in the mountains and plains of northern Italy so difficult. By 21 September 1944, Canadian troops had captured Rimini on the Adriatic, but with the difficulties of winter, it was not until the spring of 1945 that the Allies finally broke out and captured the Po Valley to the north of the Gothic line. The Germans infantry had done their job of delaying the advance up the Italian peninsula until the war's end. Perhaps the most impressive aspect of the campaign had been the German soldier's skill in defensive holding actions, despite highly unfavourable battlefield odds.

Normandy 1944

From late 1943 until June 1944, the previously neglected German Army in the West (the *Westheer*) worked with feverish zeal to strengthen the Atlantic Wall defences along the French and Belgian coasts. The Germans expected that the long-awaited Allied invasion of Nazi-occupied France was now imminent, but did not know when or where the Allies would land. Throughout spring 1944, this question dominated the thoughts of the hundreds of thousands of German soldiers manning the strong-points and slit-trenches of the supposedly impregnable 'Atlantic Wall' coastal fortifications.

In an attempt to answer this question throughout late spring 1944, thousands of German soldiers – usually the best marksmen in each unit – participated in a particular form of intelligence gathering. The French Resistance had long used pigeons to carry messages across the Channel to the Allies. As the latter's invasion preparations approached their culmination, the resistance sent more and more pigeons flying across the Channel carrying the latest intelligence on German strengths, positions, logistic dumps, and so forth. The Germans hoped that these messages might indicate where and when the Allies intended to strike. For the German soldiers ordered to intercept the pigeons, this particular duty meant hour after hour of boring observation: a four-hour stint might not produce a single sighting. Even when a soldier spotted a pigeon, his chances of downing the bird remained remote. One lucky – or perhaps particularly skilled – German marksman was Sergeant

Left: A very young German soldier anxiously scans the skies from his foxhole for signs of the much-feared Allied fighter bombers.

Günther Witte of the 1262nd Army Coastal Artillery Regiment. On 4 June 1944, at Rozel on the eastern coast of the Cotentin peninsula, Witte successfully bagged a carrier-pigeon. Attached to its legs was a tiny metal capsule, and inside, on a scrap of rice paper, was a coded message with the latest German dispositions in the Cotentin. By the next morning, the message was on the desk of Major Friedrich Hayn, intelligence officer with the LXXXIV Corps, at his Corps headquarters at St Lo. Hayn intended to show the capsule to his corps commander, General Marcks, the next day, but by that time he was too busy dealing with the actual invasion!

Rommel arrives

In early 1944, with the arrival of Field Marshal Erwin Rommel to command the German Army Group B deployed in Northern France, preparations to repel the invasion accelerated. One of Rommel's first orders was to curtail Army Group B's training so that his forces could concentrate their efforts on strengthening the beach defences. Rommel, who knew from bitter experience the potency of Allied air power, intended to stop the invasion on the beaches on the first day of the landings while the Allies remained vulnerable. But when Rommel arrived in early 1944, the Atlantic Wall existed in only a few, select locations, most notably along the Pas de Calais. During the spring, Rommel began to suspect that the Allies might land instead in Normandy, and relentlessly drove his forces to strengthen the coastal fortifications of Normandy and Brittany.

Rommel was so determined to strengthen these defences that he even ordered junior officers to participate in this effort alongside their troops. During his many inspection tours, the Field Marshal increasingly became exasperated at the inadequate defences he viewed. This was the case during his 11 May 1944 inspection of strong-point W5, located on the east coast of the Cotentin peninsula some 6.4km (4 miles) north of

Left: German grenadiers move through the devastated streets of the city of Caen. Allied heavy bombers had turned the city to rubble.

Carentan. The W5 position constituted a platoon-sized defensive locality manned by troops of the static 709th Infantry Division. Rommel's bad mood increased throughout the tour as he constantly came across positions that lacked the level of protection he required. Everywhere he discovered too few wire obstacles, insufficient mines, and inadequate numbers of reserve trenches for the positions.

Rommel finally unleashed his pent-up anger at the commander of strong-point W5, *Leutnant* (Second Lieutenant) Arthur Jahnke. Rommel demanded that Jahnke remove his suede officer's gloves, expecting to find the smooth and un-broken skin of an officer who had not joined his men in laying the strong-point's barbed wire defences. But when Jahnke – an Eastern Front veteran and holder of the coveted Knight's Cross – removed his gloves, Rommel could see that they were badly cut and grazed from Jahnke's personal toil. The Field Marshal's anger abated at the sight and instead, he had to commend Jahnke for his diligence.

In the weeks prior to the 6 June D-Day landings, the German defenders' time was fully occupied with either laborious work preparing defences, or boring hours of watch-duty during which they manned the periscopes and observation towers dotted along the French coast. When these duties had been completed, the soldiers sometimes managed to snatch some rest and relaxation. During these infrequent opportunities, soldiers often got together in their bunkers to sing a recent hit – a song called 'Cute Little Bus Conductress' – to the accompaniment of mouth-organs. These sessions were lubricated by conspicuous consumption of the local Norman speciality, Calvados, an apple-schnapps of prodigious strength. At these sessions, soldiers sometimes also (illegally) tuned their radios into Allied propaganda stations, despite the risk of severe penalties if discovered. These stations gave rather more realistic and graphic descriptions of the course of the war, in comparison with the sanitised official *Wehrmacht* reports; more importantly, the Allied stations invariably played good jazz songs between the news broadcasts.

Among the lucky German troops who served under relaxed and easy-going junior officers in their billets in Norman hamlets, there were many who decided to enjoy life as much as possible – since in a few weeks they might all be dead – despite Rommel's efforts to drive them relentlessly in preparation for the Allied landings. Even though Rommel had stepped up the pace of readiness, many German units retained a decidedly peacetime attitude right up to the invasion. When *Leutnant* (Second-Lieutenant) Arthur Jahnke arrived from the Eastern Front in spring 1944 to take over strong-point W5, he was horrified to find that French fishermen still used the road that crossed W5 in order to get to the sea. Jahnke promptly banned this practice. The Allied landings on 6 June 1944 came as a shock to many German soldiers in the West, not least because the poor weather conditions had led the German High Command to conclude that the Allies would not land that week. Indeed, just as the first Allied transport ships put to sea, many senior commanders in the Army Group B, Rommel included, were snatching quick spells of leave, or else were attending a map exercise at Rennes in Brittany.

The hell of Omaha

On D-Day, 6 June 1944, five Allied divisions landed on five invasions beaches – Sword, Juno, Gold, Omaha and Utah – across a 64-km (40-mile) sector of the Normandy coast. In addition, American and British airborne forces landed on both flanks to secure key bridges against German counter-attack. The vast majority of these intricately-planned missions were accomplished safely and, by midnight on 6 June, the Allies had secured three beachheads up to a depth of 16km (10 miles). Only at Omaha beach, the eastern-most of the two beaches at which American forces landed, did the Allied amphibious landings

Below: A Panzer IV Model G tank, well-camouflaged by foliage and protected by the building and the trees, assumes an ambush position.

experience real set-backs. Omaha beach lay 14.5km (9 miles) west of the British Gold beach, and extended some 6.4km (4 miles) from Port en Bessin in the east to Vierville in the west. Here the Americans landed elements of the 1st and 29th US Infantry Divisions.

The terrain at Omaha was problematic, because the steep bluffs behind the beach channelled any Allied advance into five obvious draws. The Germans covered each of these draws with strong-points numbered WN58 to WN62. At dawn on 6 June, at strong-point WN62, just west of the village of St Laurent, *Gefreiter* (Lance-Corporal) Hein Severloh was on observation watch. Suddenly, to his utter astonishment, the horizon filled with many hundreds of Allied ships of all shapes and sizes. Severloh complained to *Unteroffizier* (Sergeant) Krone next to him about the stupidity of the German naval coastal artillery gunners at nearby Port en Bessin who kept firing identification flares into the sky to check if the fleet was in fact German. How could it be, Severloh commented, since there were several thousand ships in the vast naval armada before their eyes? The German navy simply could not put that number to sea at once, even if it concentrated all its vessels in one spot!

Just then the 19 defenders of strong-point WN62 heard the ominous noise of Allied bombers approaching above the low cloud-cover. Instantly, they dived for cover in nearby bunkers and slit trenches. Incredibly, while the deafening inferno of exploding bombs erupted all around them, only two bombs actually fell within the strong-point. An extremely relieved *Unteroffizier* (Sergeant) Meyer concluded that the Allies must have been after targets further inland. Little did he know how close his comrades had been to death. A wave of 329 American B-29 bombers had just passed over and indeed their mission had to been to obliterate the German coastal defences at Omaha, including WN62, with 13,000 bombs. What saved the defenders was the fact that, because of the poor weather, the Allied bombers had to aim blind, using just their instruments. At the last moment, just as the bombers reached the end of their meticulously calculated run, the

Above: The crew of a 10.5cm light field howitzer prepare to fire their heavily-camouflaged gun in the narrow streets of Cherbourg, late June 1944.

Allied air commanders lost their nerve over the risk of a 'blue-on-blue' incident: that the B-29s might unleash their deadly bombs right on top of the invasion fleet. The Air High Command ordered the bomber crews to postpone their timed drop by just three seconds but this brief delay was enough to ensure that most of the bombs dropped behind the German coastal strong-points.

After the German troops had recovered from the shock of this near miss, they saw the Allied invasion armada approach the beach opposite them. Severloh watched, fascinated, as the first wave of landing craft neared the beach; surely, he pondered, the Americans were not going to land right in front of their poised muzzles? Also obvious to the defenders of WN62 was the relative lack of fire support for the first wave of American assault troops then coming into land. At that moment, neither Krone nor Severloh could have known that, because of the poor visibility, Allied commanders – again fearing 'blue-on-blue' casualties – had redirected their tactical air support onto German targets deeper in the hinterland. The problems caused by inadequate Allied fire support on Omaha were compounded by greater-than-expected German troop densities, since Allied intelligence had failed to detect the arrival of the German 352nd Infantry Division in this sector of Normandy.

The American troops disembarked into neck-deep, heavily pitching water, and struggled with heavy combat packs until they reached the beach. Severloh and his comrades patiently held their fire until the first wave of assault infantry emerged out of the water into a hail of lethal lead. Within minutes, the German defenders had decimated the lead American waves, and forced the stunned survivors to seek shelter in shallow sand-scrapes, or behind obstacles, desperately attempting to stay alive. Only a few American soldiers managed to reach the sea wall, where they huddled in relative safety. By noon, fierce German resistance along the entire Omaha sector had left 1100 American soldiers or wounded on the beach. For a while, Severloh and the troops of WN62 began to hope that their resistance might prevent the Americans from maintaining any foothold on German-occupied French soil. During the afternoon, however, many of Severloh's fellow defenders were killed or wounded as massive Allied firepower increasingly made its mark on the battle. Next, Severloh received minor injuries when Allied fire destroyed his MG 42 machine gun, and by late afternoon he and the five soldiers still alive retreated from the certain death that awaited them had they stayed in the cratered remains of their strong-point. At Omaha, the Germans, despite their earlier opportunities, had failed to prevent the successful Allied invasion of Normandy.

The siege of Cherbourg

During the last two weeks of June 1944, the Americans steadily advanced from their Utah beachhead up the Cotentin Peninsula to capture the vital port of Cherbourg. Cherbourg had been transformed into a powerful fortress with several large-calibre coastal batteries and strong concrete fortifications. Unfortunately most of these faced seaward, preventing a direct amphibious assault along the lines of the 1942 Dieppe raid. To the landward, Cherbourg was far more vulnerable and weakly defended, and it was from this direction that the Americans attacked. By 22 June, the Americans had closed to within 6.5km (4 miles) of the city and penetrated its outer defence line in several places. As the Americans approached the city suburbs on 24 June, Hitler again reiterated his orders that 'Fortress Cherbourg' be held to the last man.

By 25 June, at the Octeville headquarters of the Cherbourg garrison commander, *Generalleutnant* (Lieutenant-General) Schlieben, further resistance seemed futile, but the general's military oath bound him to carry out Hitler's orders. To the motley collection of 900 wounded Luftwaffe ground crews, naval gunners, and Organisation 'Todt' fortification workers who packed the subterranean, smoke-filled galleries at Octeville, only one question filled their minds: would Schlieben give up the pointless defence of the doomed port? As they pondered this, they could hear detonations rumbling through the galleries as the American engineers on the ground above them began to dig holes into the earth into which they packed explosives. These explosives would blow away the top of the command centre. To make matters worse, an Allied naval armada had just arrived opposite Cherbourg and now the 380mm guns of several American *Texas*-class battleships had opened up on Schlieben's underground headquarters. In desperation, the Germans ordered their still-operational 250mm artillery batteries 16km (10 miles) to the north-west on the Cap de la Hague peninsula to open fire on top of the underground headquarters complex to dislodge the Americans, but the damaged Cap de la Hague guns proved incapable of carrying out the order.

That afternoon the Americans sent a surrender request to Schlieben under a white flag,

Above: German troops, one holding a Panzerfaust disposable personal anti-tank weapon, confer on the platform of Argentan station in July 1944.

but the commander stalled in order to buy time to complete the demolition of Cherbourg's extensive port facilities. By 1932 hours on 25 July, as American infantry began to advance into Octeville's northern galleries, Schlieben sent his last message to Rommel – 'General joining troops in hand-to-hand fighting' – and picked up a carbine and headed towards the sound of gunfire. By noon the next day, several hundred of the 900 wounded that packed the complex had died due to inhalation of smoke which had been pumped into the ventilation shafts by the Americans. To make matters worse, the medics in Octeville had exhausted all their medical supplies, and American assault troops had successfully pushed deeper into the underground complex. These developments proved the last straw for Schlieben who, despite the Führer's orders, instructed his troops at Octeville to lay down their weapons to

avoid further bloodshed. Resistance continued in other parts of the town for another two days. When Cherbourg finally fell on 28 June, some 15,000 bedraggled German troops marched into Allied captivity. The Allies had successfully captured the major port they so badly needed for the daily delivery of vital logistical supplies.

Threat from the air

The fighting that raged around Cherbourg, as well as that throughout Normandy campaign, highlighted one of the most noticeable aspects of the German soldiers' experience during the summer of 1944: the devastating impact that Allied tactical and strategic air power exerted. Even before the invasion had started, the Allied aerial interdiction campaign by strategic bombers had so devastated the French rail network that on the eve of D-Day, some 1700 German military trains were delayed on route to their destinations, including that carrying *Schütze* (Private) Otto Elfeldt back to Normandy after his convalescence at a hospital near Nancy.

The terrible suffering inflicted by Allied tactical air power on the German troops in Normandy manifested itself within days of the D-Day landings. Perhaps the first portend of things to come was the nightmare trek of the *Panzer Lehr* (Demonstration) Division. On D-Day, the *Panzer Lehr* constituted the most powerful German formation in the West. This division, commanded by *Generalleutnant* (Lieutenant-General) Fritz Bayerlein, formed part of the German Strategic Reserve and was positioned around Alencon, some 120km (75 miles) south-west of Paris. On the evening of 6 June, Hitler belatedly authorised the redeployment of Bayerlein's division. During the morning of 6 June, no senior officer at the Führer's Headquarters at Rastenburg, East Prussia, had dared to wake the sleeping Hitler with the news of the Normandy invasion. The powerful *Panzer Lehr* hence commenced its approach march from Alencon to the front during the early hours of the 7th, but then was ordered to continue during daylight, despite Bayerlein's request that he move only at night.

In an attempt to minimise the losses likely from Allied fighter-bomber attacks, the division advanced in widely separated march columns with tanks interspersed with flak half-tracks. However, throughout most of the morning, repeated Allied fighter-bomber attacks ravaged Bayerlein's armoured columns. Time and time again, groups of Typhoon aircraft circled overhead before swinging down to hit the armoured columns with rockets and machine-gun fire. As soon as the tanks' observers spotted low-flying Allied aircraft approaching, all the vehicles in a column screeched to a halt, and the crews leaped into the ditches that ran along both sides of the Norman roads. All the German troops could do was claw themselves deeper into the damp French soil as the Typhoons made sweep after sweep along the column, releasing their deadly rockets and strafing anything that moved with 20mm cannon fire. Only when the column was a smoking and charred wreck did the Typhoons head off for fresh targets.

The few brave – or perhaps foolhardy – troops who continued to man their machine guns or anti-aircraft cannon in the face of these repeated attacks learned the hard way that to attempt to resist Allied air power was suicidal. The fighter aircraft *Luftflotte* 3, approximately 30 of which managed to get into the air to contest Allied air superiority, also came to the same conclusion. With strength ratios of up to 30:1, it was tantamount to suicide to attempt more than hit-and-run missions under favourable circumstances: consequently the German soldiers at the front were left entirely at the mercy of Allied tactical air power. The Tiger tanks of Michael Wittmann's 1st Company, 101st SS Heavy Tank Battalion soon developed their own unique tactics to escape the Allied air threat. When their look-outs spotted an approaching Allied Typhoon, they halted the tank, depressed the gun fully and pointed it to one side, opened every hatch, and released smoke; the Allied aircraft on most of these

Right: A King Tiger tank of the 1st Company of the German Army's 503rd Heavy Tank Battalion site concealed in a French wood.

occasions concluded that the tank had already been abandoned and disabled by its crew, and moved on to fresh targets.

Increasing numbers of anti-aircraft half-tracks, and later flakpanzers, entered German service from late 1943, in response to the increasing air superiority the Allies enjoyed. One such vehicle was the Sdkfz 7/1, a Krauss-Maffei half-track that mounted a quad 20mm *Flakvierling* 38 gun. These self-propelled flak vehicles were issued mainly to the anti-aircraft companies of *panzergrenadier* regiments and provided intimate cover against low-flying aircraft for mixed columns of tanks and APCs. The approach march of the 2nd SS Panzer Division *Das Reich* towards the Normandy front in mid-June 1944 reveals a text-book use of these anti-aircraft assets, but this relied as much as on good fortune. The division's Panther tanks proceeded in dispersed columns, the tanks separated from each other by a gap of 50m (164ft). After about 10 tanks, a Sdkfz 7/1 half-

Above: Three German soldiers who have been encircled in the Falaise pocket contemplate what fate has in store for them.

track was positioned to provide cover against low flying enemy aircraft.

Inevitably, once the weather cleared as the division approached Periers, a group of American Thunderbolt fighter-bombers strafed the column at low level and came round for a second attack. Several Sdkfz 7/1 self-propelled flak guns drove onto the roadside verge and opened fire with their four-barrelled weapons, sending hundreds of 20mm cannon rounds into the sky. Almost immediately, one Thunderbolt shuddered as it ran into the hail of fire, before plunging down to crash into a nearby wood. The other fighter-bombers abandoned their attacks in the face of this heavy defensive fire and flew off in search of easier targets. The Sdkfz 7/1 had won this particular engagement, but the scenario would be repeated hundreds of times during the

Normandy campaign. In the vast majority of cases, it was the half-tracked flak that ended up destroyed and its crews killed or wounded for their valiant efforts to resist the overwhelming air superiority the Allies enjoyed in the West, in stark contrast to the campaigns of 1940.

Artillery and strategic bombers

The German soldier in Normandy also had another threat to deal with: the use of strategic bombers employed in direct support of land operations to augment preliminary artillery bombardments. The Anglo-Canadian offensive to capture northern part of Caen, Operation 'Charnwood', was the first to employ strategic bombers in such a role. The combination of carpet bombing and intense artillery fire-plans was truly devastating. On 18 July 1944, the first morning of the Allied 'Goodwood' offensive, preliminary attacks by 2000 Allied bombers and 700 artillery pieces devastated the forward German defences with an incredible inferno of exploding

metal. One private in a Tiger crew of *Leutnant* (Second Lieutenant) Baron von Rosen's company of the 503rd Heavy Tank Battalion was literally driven insane after enduring what seemed an agonisingly long inferno of noise, light and explosions. A further two soldiers among his tank crews were driven to despair by the impact of this combined bomber-cum-artillery bombardment and blew their own brains out rather than continue to endure the torrent of deadly metal. Even von Rosen's massive, 55-ton Tigers proved vulnerable to such enormous Allied firepower, the blast of one explosion catapulting one tank into the air before it landed turret-down on the shell-holed earth; it took von Rosen's men three hours to open the turret hatch and rescue the three shaken surviving members of the crew that had been trapped inside.

Below: The crew of an assault gun load their vehicle with fresh 75cm rounds from a nearby truck in preparation for Operation 'Lüttich'.

Falaise

In late July 1944, the American 'Cobra' offensive successfully broke through the German defensive crust and their armour raced in all directions. Operation 'Lüttich', the German counter-stroke designed to seal the American penetration, failed. By mid-August, much of the German Army Group B found itself faced with encirclement in a vast pocket around Falaise. To close the gap between the British forces heading south, and the American forces advancing north toward Argentan, on 8 August General Montgomery launched a Canadian armoured thrust down the Caen-Falaise road. *Schütze* (Private) Hans Lindemann of the 89th Division remembered that, despite numerical inferiority, staunch resis-

tance by small German combat teams north of Falaise managed to prevent the Allies from meeting up at Chambois and sealing the pocket until 19 August. By then the battered remnants of 20 German Divisions were racing east in order to escape encirclement in the pocket. The Germans launched a relief effort from outside the pocket, as, meanwhile, disorganised German battle groups within the pocket – like that of paratrooper Heinz Knaust – launched themselves in frenzied attacks against the Allied blocking positions established at Trun. The tired, bedraggled and desperate soldiers within dozens of these German battle groups advanced down narrow, sunken Norman lanes and smashed their way through the Allied blocking positions to

Left: The pocket of death. As the German forces surrounded in the Falaise pocket tried to break out, Allied tactical air power inflicted terrible damage on both personnel and equipment. Here victims of an air attack have been cleared off the road with their equipment. Allied air superiority was complete by the time of the Normandy landings, which allowed the Allies to delay and harass the reinforcements sent to the front, as well as destroying any German strong-points or pockets of resistance. The German troops learnt to move at night or under cover, so great was the threat from the air.

safety outside of the encirclement. In total, 40,000 of the 100,000 encircled German troops managed to escape the hell of Falaise. However, as these desperate German forces attempted to break out, the Allies unleashed the full power of their tactical air forces in ceaseless daytime sorties, wreaking terrible damage on German equipment and personnel. Only three of Knaust's platoon managed to reach safety, and all had been wounded. By 23 August, German resistance in the pocket had finished. When Allied troops inspected the carnage inflicted by their firepower on German soldiers, they were appalled; dead horses lay everywhere, bloated in the sun, together with the corpses of dead soldiers and wrecked military equipment of all types.

After the end of resistance at Falaise, the *Westheer* beat a full-scale retreat as it sought to escape envelopment in a second, larger, Allied pocket against the River Seine. The Germans suffered heavy losses during their daytime retreat, thanks to Allied air attack, while chronic fuel shortages forced them to abandon most of their remaining vehicles. During 25–29 August, they improvised a ferrying operation for their forces across the Seine, and then continued towards the borders of the Reich. During 80 days of intense combat in Normandy, the German Army Group B had been decimated, having lost 1400 AFVs and suffered 600,000 personnel casualties. The *Westheer* had suffered a momentous strategic disaster in the West.

North-West Europe 1944–45

The post-Normandy north-west Europe campaign lasted from the flight of the *Westheer* back across the Seine in late August 1944, to the German surrender in early May 1945. During this period, German troops – infantrymen, panzer crews, paratroopers and commandos – faced a wide variety of experiences. They fought desperate rearguard actions to stem the almost remorseless Allied advance, sometimes amid the concrete bunkers of fortifications. These soldiers also witnessed the chaos of a broken army in flight, participated in the improvised defensive counter-strokes against Allied airborne forces dropped in their rear, and even, on one occasion, took part in an ambitious offensive conducted with meagre resources.

Retreat

During the first week of September 1944, the German Army continued its headlong, disorganised retreat from France into Belgium. Only a relatively small number of units retained their cohesion, *Oberst* (Colonel) Ritgen of the 'Panzer Lehr' recalled, and these fought stubborn defensive rearguards to protect less mobile formations. On 7 September at Briey, south of Metz, for example, a company-sized detachment of the

Left: German grenadiers advance past burning vehicles during the surprise counter-offensive through the Ardennes in December 1944.

Above: Scratch German forces, such as these Kar 98-equipped infantrymen, were used against the Allied paratroop landings in September 1944.

Panzer Lehr division burst forwards to throw the Americans out of the village. During combat at close quarters within the village, tank driver Reinhold Schneider even rammed enemy artillery pieces against a wall with his tank. But these exceptions aside, behind these valiant rear-guards many German soldiers witnessed evidence that the normally impressive German military discipline was close to collapse. One infantryman, Karl-Ludwig Opitz, remembered vividly the signs of chaos that confronted him. As his unit pulled back, he frequently saw lorries abandoned at the road-side after they had run out of petrol; a grenade in the engine was sufficient to stop the Allies from utilising them. Opitz also witnessed heavily laden staff cars, full of officer's possessions, desperately fighting their way through the throngs of vehicles, marching infantry and civilians, all heading north and north-east away from the approaching Allied advance. Opitz even recalled seeing rear-echelon troops jogging down roads pushing prams filled with loot – fine wines, joints of meat, paintings – while others stole civilian clothes at gun-point from the locals to cover their attempt to desert from what they now believed was a beaten army.

Arnhem

Unhappily for the Allies, the disintegration evident within the Westheer was to prove short-lived. After 9 September 1944, the Germans managed to improvise a cohesive, but thin defensive crust as the momentum of the Allied advance stumbled, due primarily to logistic deficiencies. But within a week the determined German soldiers in their foxholes and slit trenches soon faced another threat: the landing of Allied airborne forces behind the frontline. In attempt to kick-start the faltering Allied advance, Field Marshal Montgomery launched

Operation 'Market-Garden', an atypically audacious offensive aimed to 'bounce' the River Rhine before the Germans recovered their cohesion. Montgomery ordered parachute forces to land at key communication nodes behind the lines and wait until General Horrocks' XXX Corps advanced through Holland to link up with them. At the northern drop zone, Montgomery ordered the paras of the British 1st Airborne Division to seize the bridge at Arnhem and hold it for three days until Horrocks' armour relieved them.

In the Arnhem area prior to 17 September 1944, the Germans had managed to shore up their frontline by drafting in large numbers of poorly trained personnel from the German Navy and Air Force to form the newly raised First Parachute Army. *Oberleutnant* (Lieutenant) Heinz Volz of the hastily improvised Parachute Regiment 'von Hoffman' recalled vividly what inadequate training these troops possessed. One morning, at the regiment's assembly area near Tilburg, Volz was demonstrating how the Panzerfaust anti-tank weapon ought to be employed. One NCO, just transferred from the *Luftwaffe*, picked up the weapon and accidently discharged it straight into a nearby ammunition dump. Luckily the projectile did not cause the dump to explode because the equally untrained armourer had primed the weapon incorrectly. In addition to lack of training, many of these troops only possessed outdated or captured weapons, and wore assorted uniforms: the demoted former officers of the *Luftwaffe* Penal Battalion 6, for instance, wore tropical uniforms last used by the *Afrika Korps* in 1942!

It was a clear, sunny day on 17 September, and this made the appearance of a strange weather phenomenon all the more puzzling to the German soldiers who witnessed it. Hans Moeller of the engineer battalion of the 9th SS Panzer Division *Hohenstaufen* was perplexed when the clear, blue sky began to fill with endless numbers of small, white clouds. At St Joseph's School in Arnhem 3.2km (2 miles) away, *Oberleutnant* (Lieutenant) Enthammer of the V2 rocket artillery unit saw the same phenomenon and initially thought that he was witnessing snow. Within seconds, how-

ever, Moeller decided that the white blobs were not cirrocumulus clouds, while Enthammer rationalised that it never snowed in Holland during September. Both then reached the same conclusion: that they were witnessing the landing of a vast Allied paratrooper force many miles behind the front line.

As the white Allied parachutes floated toward the ground, German forces immediately began to move towards the sounds of gunfire. At the Harskamp training centre, *panzergrenadiers* of the 9th SS Division had already packed their equipment into the lorries earmarked to take them to the nearby railway for redeployment to the Reich. Just at that moment, news of the landing reached them. *SS-Rottenführer* (Corporal) Paul Mueller remembered that the troops grabbed rifles and a few handfuls of ammunition which they stuffed into their pockets, as their ammunition pouches were buried deep in the packed lorries. Minus their steel helmets, also buried deep inside the trucks, they began to jog toward the spot where the British paratroopers had landed. Some 40.2km (25 miles) to the north at Deventer, *SS-Rottenführer* (Corporal) Rudolf Trapp's 50 man-strong *panzergrenadier* company of the 10th SS Panzer Division *Frundsberg* had witnessed the over-flight of hundreds of Allied transport aircraft. Without waiting for orders, they mounted their requisitioned bicycles – all their vehicles had been lost in the desperate retreat from France – and pedalled furiously toward Arnhem. Within two hours, Trapp's soldiers were fighting the British airborne forces.

On the afternoon of 17 September Lieutenant-Colonel Frost's 2nd Parachute Battalion advanced through Oosterbeek and into the outskirts of Arnhem. The British soldiers advanced cautiously through the narrow streets to close on their objective, the Arnhem road bridge. As the British paras approached the bridge around 1800 hours, they witnessed the 40 armoured vehicles of the 9th SS Reconnaissance Battalion thunder unchallenged across the bridge and head south toward Nijmegen. Armoured car driver *SS-Panzerschütze* (Private) Hans Weber recollected how, three hours previously, the Knight's Cross award ceremony for *SS-Hauptsturmführer* (Captain) Viktor Gräbner – the battalion's commander – had been interrupted when the immense Allied airborne armada flew overhead. As white parachutes came into view in the sky above, Gräbner received orders to reconnoitre south toward Nijmegen.

Some 30 minutes after Gräbner's battalion had crossed Arnhem bridge, the following unit – a company of the 10th SS Reconnaissance Battalion – ran into a surprise attack by the Frost's paratroopers who seized control of the bridge. After moving down from the north, the 50 troopers of Rudolf Trapp's SS company approached the British positions on the bridge just as twilight set in. Hugging the buildings for cover, Trapp's men pushed on until British small-arms fire began to take its toll on the advancing Germans. The SS soldiers now changed their tactics, moving laterally to clear the buildings situated around the northern bridge ramp. As they cleared each building in turn, they searched

feverishly for discarded British weapons, for the men possessed virtually no ammunition for their Karabiner 98 rifles; Sten guns were particularly coveted, Trapp recalled. While this encounter raged around the bridge, at Nijmegen Gräbner had finally heard that the bridge had fallen, and immediately dashed back to Arnhem.

That same afternoon and early evening, to the north-west of Frost's force, the rest of the British 1st Parachute Brigade completed the task of consolidating its landing zones around Ginkel Heath near Oosterbeek. Next, as the British soldiers began pushing east toward northern suburbs of Arnhem, they encountered stiff resistance from scratch enemy forces such as SS Training Battalion *Krafft* and the Blocking Group *Spindler*. One force the Germans swiftly mobilised to deal with the western flank of the

Below: German soldiers dug camouflaged fox-holes on the edges of Ginkel Heath to contain the British 1st Airborne Division's landings.

British perimeter at Oosterbeek was the aspirant-NCOs of the SS School *Arnheim*, commanded by *SS-Standartenführer* (Colonel) Lippert. To secure some mobility for their hastily assembled scratch force, the school's aspirants seized every conceivable form of transport by force from the local population, including dozens of bicycles, eight horse-drawn carts, and even two fire engines. One *SS-Schütze* (Private) recalled that they even seized two wood-burning lorries, but these soon broke down as no one really understood how to operate them. Late that afternoon, Lippert's men joined the uncoordinated, piecemeal attacks launched by the rag-tag units of the improvised Division *von Tettau* against the western British defensive line. The soldiers of the Dutch SS Surveillance Battalion 3, commanded by *SS-Hauptsturmführer* (Captain) Anton Helle, exceeded the levels of incompetence displayed by many of General von Tettau's untrained units.

Above: German infantry, supported by armour, advance down a road in Arnhem to tighten their encirclement of the paratroopers on the bridge.

Helle committed his four companies in a piecemeal and uncoordinated fashion, all of which suffered heavily at the hands of the skilled British paras. The first of Helle's battalion to arrive was the band, which possessed a few lorries since it had recently fulfilled the tactical role of a rapid reaction force to collect Allied airmen downed behind German lines. Without any reconnaissance, the inexperienced bandsmen simply advanced into a British ambush and were mown down by British small-arms fire. Some of the survivors promptly took the opportunity presented by the band's disorganised flight to desert by changing into civilian clothes in the nearest hamlet. Yet despite the unimpressive manner in which these attacks were launched, the hastily assembled German forces nevertheless managed to exert strong pressure on the British perimeter.

The following morning of 18 September, Gräbner – in typical SS style – attempted a surprise *coup-de-main* to retake the Arnhem bridge from the south. At 0900 hours, his own vehicle – the British Humber armoured car he had captured in Normandy – led his battalion's 22 armoured cars and APCs in a dash across the bridge. Gräbner hoped that the sight of the Humber might fool Frost's paratroopers into thinking that the approaching column was in fact the British XXX Corps come to relieve them. Gräbner's Humber rushed onto the bridge but the British, after initial hesitation, rumbled his ploy and opened up with PIAT anti-tank rounds, hand grenades and mortar rounds. Hans Weber remembered the inferno of fire that rapidly knocked out six of the armoured cars on the bridge. As the driver crawled to safety beyond the far end of the bridge, he saw the unmistakable figure of his battalion commander fall fatally wounded on to the bridge decking.

With Gräbner's attack thwarted, the British consolidated their positions and waited for XXX Corps to arrive. All through the next day, and the one after that, intensive German attacks, backed by intense artillery, slowly whittled down Frost's defensive perimeter and inflicted ever higher casualties. After four days' heroic resistance, and with the British ground forces still miles away, the exhausted remnants of Frost's force surrendered to the enemy.

The full fury of German attacks then shifted to the remainder of the 1st Airborne Division at Oosterbeek. By now, Allied tactical air power was reasserting itself on the battlefield. North of the Oosterbeek perimeter, for example, Alfred Ziegler of the 9th SS Anti-tank Battalion recalled a devastating attack by British Mosquito fighter-bombers against their flak positions. After two passes, Ziegler remembered, the dreaded Allied 'Jabos' (fighter-bombers) left nothing standing. But Allied air power alone could not save the rest of the 1st Airborne Division from the powerful German counter-attacks. Instead, the remnants of the British airborne division were forced to

Right: The elite grenadiers of the II-SS Panzer Corps were so impressed with the incredible resistance put up by Frost's paratroopers despite their lack of support and heavy equipment that they treated their prisoners with great respect. Here two paratroopers help their injured colleague. The armoured vehicle is an assault gun, which mounted a large calibre weapon but had no turret, to save weight and lower its profile. They were increasingly used in an anti-tank role, for which they were well suited. Their only real disadvantage was the lack of traverse for the gun, which meant that the whole vehicle had to be moved if the target was not directly in front of it.

retreat back across the River Neder Rijn to the safety of Allied lines. Desperate German defensive improvisation had halted Montgomery's 'Market-Garden' gamble.

The Battle of the Bulge

Although the experiences of German soldiers during this campaign remained dominated by withdrawals, rearguard actions, defensive missions, and local counter-strikes such as at Arnhem, German troops also participated in offensive operations. German soldiers fought in corps-sized counter-strikes, such as that at Meijel during the night of 26/27 October 1944. However,

the only major counter-offensive the Germans conducted during the campaign was their mid-December Ardennes operation, commonly known as 'the Battle of the Bulge'. On 16 September 1944, the day before 'Market-Garden' commenced, Hitler reached a momentous decision: soon his forces would launch a counter-offensive that would transform the course of the war in the West. He decided that they would attack in the rugged, hilly and densely wooded terrain of the Ardennes, since its unsuitability for mechanised warfare meant that the Americans deployed only weak defences in this sector. Hitler insisted that the soldiers participating in the offensive strive

to advance 153km (95 miles) to seize the vital port of Antwerp, but this proved far too ambitious, given the limited resources available.

On 16 December 1944, the soldiers of Field Marshal Walther Model's Army Group B began the counter-offensive amid a spell of bad weather which kept the Allies' awesome air power at bay. For many of the German soldiers involved in the attack, the overriding characteristic of their experiences was one of desperate improvisation. Logistical supplies like munitions and rations remained utterly inadequate for an operation of this scale, and the attacking Germans forces in particular remained critically short of fuel.

Consequently, soldiers like *Oberschütze* (Private) Werner Persin of the *Panzer Lehr* Division went into combat with rubber tubes to siphon off petrol from any Allied vehicles they encountered *en route*. Just to keep the attack going, the troops of the lead panzer divisions recognised, they had to capture several Allied fuel dumps in order to keep themselves supplied with petrol!

Covert operations

Given the meagre resources available to the Germans during the Ardennes counter-offensive, Hitler ordered that small numbers of the troops involved conduct special, covert operations to increase the likelihood of German success. One such mission, Operation 'Griffin', involved the troops of the 150th Panzer Brigade, commanded by *SS-Standartenführer* (Colonel) Otto Skorzeny. Skorzeny was Hitler's favourite commando officer after his spectacularly successful September 1943 airborne raid which had rescued Mussolini from Allied captivity on Gran Sasso mountain. For the Ardennes offensive, Hitler ordered Skorzeny's troops – wearing American uniforms and driving captured Allied vehicles – to infiltrate behind the lines during the confusion created by the initial German attack. Some of the brigade's soldiers were to seize the key Meuse bridges and hold them until the German armour arrived, while others were tasked with creating confusion and chaos behind the American front-lines. Troops dressed as American military policemen, such as *Unteroffizier* (Sergeant) Manfred Parnass, were to misdirect Allied traffic in the rear areas to hinder the arrival of Allied re-inforcements at the front.

To form Skorzeny's 150th Brigade, the High Command put out a request to all units for medically fit volunteers who were trained in individual combat techniques and who could speak English. In addition, the Germans trawled their units for captured Allied vehicles and uniforms which were sent to Skorzeny at the

Left: The Malmédy massacre: the reputation of the Waffen-SS *was tarnished again when troops of Peiper's Battle Group murdered 77 Americans.*

Grafenwöhr training grounds. By early December, the brigade had received a motley collection of Allied equipment, which included some American summer uniforms, several winter ones, but all with large German triangular prisoner of war markings on them, together with two inoperable Sherman tanks. One volunteer for the operation was *Gefreiter* (Lance-Corporal) Wilhelm Schmidt. In early November 1944 he reported to an SS training camp at Freidenthal for assessment of his linguistic abilities. He was then sent to an Allied prisoner-of-war camp at Küstrin, East Prussia, to brush up his American slang, before rejoining the brigade at Grafenwöhr. Here he received instruction in American army organisation, tactical drill, and field procedures, as well as further language training. Each soldier received an American rank, one that usually represented amazingly swift promotion. Overnight, volunteer *Gefreiter* (Lance-Corporal) Rolf Meyer, for example, became Second-Lieutenant Charlie Holtzman.

By 16 December the 150th Brigade deployed 2200 men, including a stiffening of seasoned veterans from the SS Raiding Formation Centre and the SS Parachute Battalion 600. In addition, Skorzeny's force fielded one operational Sherman, 13 specially modified Panther tanks intended to resemble the American M-10 tank destroyer, four American scout cars, 15 Dodge trucks, and sufficient small arms for just one commando company. On 16 December, the first day of the German attack, 44 commandos infiltrated Allied lines to undertake demolitions and misdirect traffic. One such infiltrator was former German naval officer, *Korvettenkapitän* von Behr, who slipped through the lines until he reached Malmédy on 17 December to undertake a reconnaissance. Although von Behr's activities aroused some suspicion among the American defenders, he managed to slip back to the German lines.

That same day, American Sergeant Ed Keoghan of the 291st Combat Engineer Battalion recalled being directed by military police – actually Skorzeny's commandos – towards what was supposed to be Waimes but turned out to be Malmédy. Also on 17 December, a jeep-mounted team of three Skorzeny commandos – *Oberfähnrich* (Sergeant) Günther Billing, *Gefreiter* (Lance-Corporal) Wilhelm Schmidt, and *Unteroffizier* (Senior Corporal) Manfred Parnass – ran into a enemy infantry patrol and were captured. Under interrogation, they 'confessed' the false intelligence that their mission was to assassinate Eisenhower, the Allied supreme commander. By 18 December, the Allied rear was awash with rumours of disguised Germans active in the area, and any American lost or perceived to be acting suspiciously was likely to be arrested or, sadly on several occasions, even shot. American troops would challenge suspects with obscure questions like what was the capital of Illinois or who was Betty Grable's current flame: the latter question stumped General Bradley when stopped at a check-point by a trooper who refused to believe that he was talking to his own army group commander.

A grim fate awaited any German commandos, like the three-man jeep team captured on 17 December, who were caught in American uniforms. This practice flouted the norms of war and left the commandos facing the prospect of being shot as spies. After an American military tribunal had examined the three men, it duly passed a death sentence on each. At the icy cold dawn of 23 December, American soldiers marched the three condemned soldiers to a wall, tied them to stakes in front of it, and then blindfolded them. Next, the 12-man execution party attached white circles to the three soldiers' tunics over their hearts and, as the American squad took aim, Senior Cadet Billing said clearly and steadily, his voice showing no emotion, 'Long live our Führer', just before the sounds of bullets rent the crisp morning air and the three slumped dead, held by their restraints to the stakes. Hence, while the 150th Brigade managed to sow confusion behind the lines, the personal cost for the soldiers involved could prove very high.

While Operation 'Griffin' was underway, *SS-Oberstgruppenführer* (Colonel-General) Dietrich's Sixth Panzer Army commenced its attack, spearheaded by troops of the SS *Leibstandarte* Division. A reinforced regiment-sized armoured force – the SS Battle Group *Peiper* – led the advance of the *Leibstandarte*. Under the command of *SS-Obersturmbannführer* (Lieutenant-Colonel) Joachim Peiper, the battle group's mission was to swiftly exploit any success and to develop the offensive towards Antwerp before the Allies could recover from the shock of the attack. During 17–19 December, Peiper's armour – a mix of Panzer IV and Panther tanks, plus some King Tigers – fought their way forwards 40km (25 miles) to Stoumont. However, it was only when Peiper's advance faltered beyond Stoumont on 20 December that 10 of his King Tigers caught up with the lighter and faster spearhead tanks.

Malmédy

On Sunday 17 December, Peiper's SS fanatics murdered 77 American prisoners at Malmédy. His men, including *SS-Sturmann* (Lance-Corporal) Goerg Fleps, had assembled in a field unarmed prisoners of the 285th Field Artillery Observation Battalion, who had been captured just east of Malmédy on the road to Thirimont. What then transpired remains shrouded in controversy, but it appears as if several jittery SS troopers, perhaps fearing an escape attempt by the prisoners, opened fire on them, and that the rest of the guards then joined in with the massacre. At the subsequent Dachau trial in 1946, an American officer who survived the atrocity identified Panzer IV driver Goerg Fleps as the first SS soldier to open fire. Whatever the cause of that first act of violence, it is clear that, after the incident, SS soldiers checked over the bodies systematically and finished off many of the wounded prisoners. The Dachau trial passed no less than 43 death sentences and 22 life imprisonments on the SS troopers involved, although many of these were subsequently commuted to lesser sentences. In a similar incident at Stavelot a few days later, German troops, including the fervent Nazi *SS-Sturmann* (Lance-Corporal) Ernst Kilat, murdered in a reprisal action some 23 civilians sheltering in a house because one American soldier also sheltering there had shot and killed an SS trooper as he advanced down a nearby road.

Above: Even young teenagers were called up into the Volksturm *(Home Guard) for one last effort to stem the Allied advance into the Reich.*

On 21 December, some four days after the Malmédy incident, Peiper's troops found themselves surrounded at La Gleize by Allied counter-strikes and were thus cut off from further logistic resupply. To make matters worse, during the next day, the mist that over the previous six days had kept Allied fighter-bombers grounded, now disappeared. *Feldwebel* (Sergeant) Karl Laun of a *Luftwaffe* flak unit attached to Peiper's battle group described vividly the last days of the doomed battle group. Throughout the night of 21/22 December, American artillery pounded the encircled positions held by Peiper's men, and throughout the day, American attacks penetrated deeper into the unit's perimeter. That evening, an air drop took place, but only a fraction of the required food and fuel was dropped within the unit's shrinking positions. In addition, an attempt to float supplies down to the now-starving men along the Ambleve River failed completely. Despite terrible hunger pains, given the intensity of enemy artillery and mortar fire, Laun dared not even attempt to grab American ration packs visible just 30m (98ft) away.

By the afternoon of 23 December, intense artillery fire had devastated Peiper's position in the village of La Gleize, and he made the decision to attempt a break out. Peiper ordered the 200 wounded men and medics to stay behind and instructed them to wait eight hours before destroying the battle group's 32 remaining operational, but fuel-less, tanks.

Meanwhile, *Feldwebel* Laun recalled, during the early hours of 24 December, 800 of Peiper's fit soldiers quietly infiltrated out through the darkness towards the nearby village of La Venne. Led by local Belgians forced to act as guides, by noon the starving and exhausted SS troopers could go no further and sought cover in a dense forest.

Feldwebel Laun and the other bedraggled soldiers grabbed some much-needed rest. With the weather cleared, it was imperative that Peiper's troops avoid detection by low-flying American aircraft. By the time they had reached the forest, many of the troops had a terrible thirst, their lips cracked and bleeding. In desperation, they tore

ice from branches, or else lapped hungrily from muddy puddles. Predictably, soldiers soon began to succumb to stomach disorders. As Peiper again pushed on his men that evening, it was evident to all that troop discipline and morale had sunk perilously low: one by one, the tired SS troopers discarded their weapons to lighten their load.

During that evening, the column pushed on, despite encountering several American outposts. An exhausted Laun remembered having to swim with his colleagues across icy streams, like the Salm at Rochelinval. Once on the other side, several soldiers could only be stopped from falling asleep where they stood by being hit awake by their colleagues. By dawn on Christmas Day, just as their last reserves of energy began to wane, Peiper's exhausted, soaked, filthy and starving troopers finally linked up with German patrols east of Wanne. With Peiper's demise came the stalling of the German northern thrust.

To the south, the Fifth Panzer Army enjoyed greater success, and at the high-point of the German advance on 23 December, the 2nd Panzer Division had pushed forward to just 6.5km (4 miles) short of the Meuse bridges. Here, its tanks, having failed to capture Allied fuel stocks, ran out of petrol. That same day, however, American forces commenced counter-attacks against the German salient which, by early January, forced the Germans back to their starting positions. During these withdrawal operations – as Jagdpanzer IV commander *SS-Unterscharführer* (Senior Corporal) Alfred Schultz of the *Hitlerjugend* recalled – Allied fighter-bombers inflicted many casualties on the retreating German armour. In retrospect, the German Ardennes counter-offensive proved to be a costly, futile, and ultimately disastrous, gamble that threw away Germany's last, precious, armoured reserves. Consequently, the badly weakened *Westheer* could field only meagre forces on the west bank of the Rhine to prevent a successful Allied advance into the heart of the Reich.

By March 1945, the Allies had successfully crossed the Rhine and now inexorably advanced across Germany in the face of dwindling German resistance. On 5 May 1945, the German forces in north-western Europe surrendered. Just three days later, a general surrender of all German forces was announced.

Left: Bedraggled German infantry shelter from the elements in a dug-out west of the Rhine, which offered little obstruction to the Allies.